EXPLORING THE TWIN CITIES WITH CHILDREN:

a selection of tours, sights,
museums, recreational activities
and many other places for
children and adults
to visit together.

Elizabeth S. French

Illustrated by Lynn B. Sandness

9th Edition

D1360592

Elizabeth S. French, the author, was a librarian and is a mother and grandmother, a former nursery school field trip organizer, Cub Scout leader and present day discoverer of new and old activities to explore with children and grandchildren. She resides in Lauderdale, Minnesota.

Lynn B. Sandness, the illustrator, is a visual artist in drawing and sculpture. His artwork is in public and private collections throughout the United States. He resides in Duluth, Minnesota.

This is a cooperative family work as author and illustrator are sister and brother.

Published by
Nodin Press, Inc., LLC
530 North Third St. Suite 120, Minneapolis, MN 55401
13 ISBN: 978-1-935666-32-5

To my grandchildren, Jack, Allie, Ryan and Chase, and to all children who are discovering the World, including the Twin Cities and the state of Minnesota, is for exploring.

As we have discovered, the World has become more and more accessible. Visit "America's Story," an Internet website for children and families [**www.americaslibrary.gov**] created by the Library of Congress. It offers discovery stories including "Explore the States." Choose Minnesota. Photos and a brief description of our state appear.

To my continuing delight, EXPLORING THE TWIN CITIES WITH CHILDREN, is now in edition nine. Many new activities have been added, previously included activities have been contacted, many visited again and all brought up-to-date. Museums, community festivals, tours, historical places and musical and art events have been added which either did not exist or had not yet been discovered in the previous editions.

The book continues to grow and change, as has the Twin Cities and beyond, through the inclusion of the many experiences offered to our young residents. It is again my wish that using this book will help children and adults continue to find and enjoy together these exciting and interesting activities in our Twin Cities area here and throughout the state.

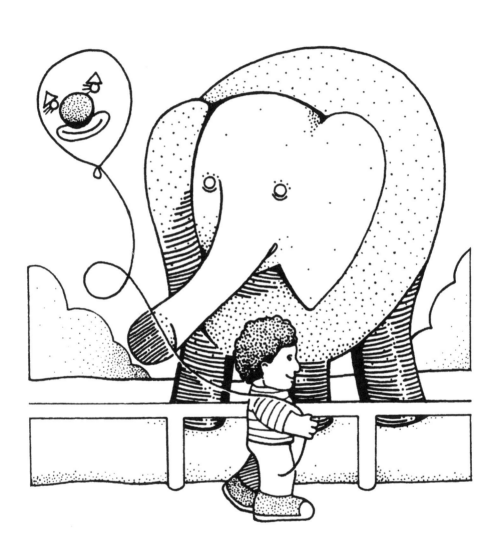

INTRODUCTION

Children love "Show and Tell." Our Twin Cities and surrounding area can be thought of as a huge "Show and Tell" for exploring. Through posters, newspapers, radio, television, people and the Internet, word of an especially fun event or place is spread. But much is missed because the announcements are not always seen or heard. Or perhaps it is not known that such places or events even exist.

This book is a guide to finding those places and events in our exciting community and beyond. It is written for adults to read and use as an aid in selecting from the many child-oriented activities not only in our area but now, throughout the state. Those included have been selected because they focus on the interests of young children...in showing them and telling them more about their world.

SUGGESTIONS

••• The book is organized alphabetically like a directory. **A CATEGORIES INDEX** is located at the end of the book. Use it to find an activity like a nature center when its name is not known.

••• An asterisk * indicates the activity has an admission fee. Some, formerly with a fee, have eliminated or lowered it.

••• Each activity has its zip code listed. Use the zip code maps for Minneapolis and St. Paul on the inside covers to find the approximate location of an activity.

••• Call or visit the activity's website before going to the activity to be sure the admission fees, hours and days open are still as listed. **THEY DO CHANGE**.

••• Internet websites for the activities are included. Look here for maps, photos, one-time happenings and newsy items.

••• Reservations are a must at some places. Make them in advance to avoid disappointments. Some require arrangements several months in advance.

••• Some places can only be visited by groups of children. Organize a neighborhood group, nursery or daycare group, Brownie or Scout group with plenty of chaperones for these outings. For very young children, one adult for every two or three children is a good idea.

••• For groups of young children, identification tags are a good idea. Make them big and all the same color. Do not include name on tag. Those that hang around the neck are especially visible.

••• Instead pin the child's name and telephone number on the **INSIDE** of a clothing item as a safety precaution in case the child becomes separated from you.

••• Most places need a bit of beforehand preparation and explaining so the child knows what to expect.

••• Visit some places like a museum or nature center frequently but for short periods of time, concentrating on seeing two or three things each time.

••• Enjoy the child enjoying an experience and enjoy it yourself.

NOTES

ALPHABETICAL INDEX

A

B

C

D

*admission or fee

E

F

G

H

I

*admission or fee

J

K

L

M

N

*admission or fee

O

P

R

S

T

*admission or fee

*admission or fee

DAY TRIPS

These activities are located outside the Twin Cities area. Because they take a longer time to travel to, it is suggested that at least a day be set aside for exploring them. Some may need a planned overnight stay. Included in this edition is an expanded selection of websites as well as updated listings of helpful regional telephone numbers and addresses for planning visits throughout Minnesota.

SEASONAL EVENTS

Some events occur for only a few days or weeks during the year. Approximate dates are given in the descriptions, but also check websites, the newspapers or call the telephone numbers listed for complete information.

SPRING

*admission or fee

SUMMER

FALL

WINTER

*admission or fee

*AAMODT'S APPLE FARM
6428 Manning Ave. N.
Stillwater, 55082

651-439-3127 (infoline)
www.aamodtsapplefarm.com

Guided school tours of the apple orchards are given to groups of children of kindergarten age through grade 5. The tours are Tuesday through Thursday beginning the week after Labor Day and continue through the 1st week in October. Children ride the tractor-pulled hay wagon into the orchard, walk through the apple cooler, see the antique kitchen and watch bees making honey. The hour long tour costs $4 per person. As the tours are very popular, reservations are a must and should be made beginning in August.

No reservations are necessary for group visits on weekends. But be aware that these days can be very crowded with lots of visitors. Upon arrival at the orchards, ask where the harvesting is taking place that day. You can now pick your own apples at Aamodt's, too. Call or visit their website to find out what varieties are available and when.

A trip to the Apple Farm has other attractions besides just enjoying the turn-of-the-century reconstructed farm setting with its rebuilt 140 year-old barn. They could include the John Deere Kiddie Trike ride and wandering through the Hay Bale Maze. Each has a small fee.

The orchards are open from August through December. Visit the website or call for the current hours. Aamodt's is located just north of Highway 36 on Manning Avenue between North St. Paul and Stillwater.

Note: Special family events are held on weekends. If the hot air balloons are launching, this is an especially awesome and colorful event to see. Visit their website **www.aamodtsballoons.com** or call (651-351-0101) for details on upcoming ones.

**What a delicious way
To spend a day!**

*ALEXANDER RAMSEY HOUSE
Minnesota Historical Society (MHS)
265 S. Exchange St. at Walnut in Irvine Park
St. Paul, 55102

651-296-8760
www.mnhs.org/places/sites/arh

This is the home of Minnesota's first territorial and second state governor. Alexander Ramsey also served the state as a U.S. senator and served our country as secretary of war. His French Renaissance-style home was built in 1872. The carriage house today serves as a gift shop and visitors center. The mansion is open for group touring throughout the year with a reservation required. Call or visit the website for current information on days and hours and tour times when open to the public as they vary with the season. Admission is $8 for adults, $6 for seniors and $5 for children ages 6 to 17. School groups are $5 per student.

Note: Call 651-296-8760 for group tour arrangements at other times throughout the year.

*AMERICAN SWEDISH INSTITUTE
2600 Park Ave. S.
Minneapolis, 55407

612-871-4907 (infoline)
www.americanswedishinst.org

The museum is housed in a beautiful 33-room mansion that looks like a castle. Children should have fun looking throughout the house for the many mythical figures such as a lion with eagle wings or a cherub with butterfly wings. Adults will marvel at the many ceramic fireplaces. On Sunday afternoons special events such as a film or lecture are held. Other seasonal events are held throughout the year. A Nordic Christmas includes a traditionally decorated Christmas tree and table settings. The museum is open Tuesday through Sunday. It is closed on Monday. Admission is $6 for adults, $5 for seniors and $4 for students 6 to 18 and free for children under 6.

School groups of 10 from first grade age and up can experience a guided tour with reservations. Contact the Youth & Family Programs Coordinator at 612-870-3374 for arrangement details.

*ANIMAL FACILITY TOURS FOR CHILDREN
University of Minnesota, St. Paul Campus
Dept. of Animal Science
305 Haecker Hall
1364 Eckles Ave.
St. Paul, 55108

612-624-2722
www.ansci.umn.edu/tours.htm

School, scout, neighborhood and others in groups of 10 or more can tour the animal barns to see and learn about beef cattle, dairy cows, calves and other animals as permitted. Guided tours led by graduate students in the Animal Science Dept. are given year round. Arrangements for a tour should be made several weeks in advance by calling weekdays between the hours of 8 AM and 4 PM. Reservations for May tours begin in March as May is such a popular month. The $2 per visitor fee supports graduate student activities.

ANIMAL HUMANE SOCIETY
845 Meadow Lane N.
Golden Valley, 55422

763-522-4325
763-489-2220 Education Dept.
www.animalhumansociety.org

Children are invited to visit the society accompanied by an adult, of course, between noon and 8 PM weekdays and 10 AM to 6 PM Saturday and Sunday. A group guided tour of the society for ages 6 and older begins with a short introductory program on who they are and what they are about. This is followed by an introduction to the many different live animals that might include rabbits, birds, puppies and kittens. A usual group tour lasts about one hour. The cost is a $1 per person. Groups of fewer than 10 pay a fee of $10. Reservations are required.

Note: Every couple of months, shelter tours for smaller groups and individuals are offered in the evening at the Golden Valley location. Cost is $1 per person and tour begins at 7 PM. Attendees must be at least 6 years old. Visit the website or call for when scheduled.

Society staff will arrange to come to schools of kindergarten age and older with humane animal workshops and programs. Programs offered include The Good Kind Giant, Pet Responsibility, Urban Wildlife, Animal Communication & Bite Prevention and Animal Related Careers and others. Cost is $50 per program. Contact the Education Dept. for scheduling and additional information.

Other learning opportunities the society offers include the PetSet Youth Club, a service learning program, for 5th through 8th grade children. There is a membership fee of $50 for each semester of this program. Summer Camps, Birthday Parties and Scouting Programs are also offered. Check the website or call for more details on these.

*ARBORETUM
University of Minnesota
3675 Arboretum Dr.
Chanhassen, 55317

952-443-1400 (infoline)
www.arboretum.umn.edu
www.arboretum.umn.edu/kidclasses.aspx

The landscape arboretum is located on 1200 acres of land in Chanhassen. There are marked trails for hiking with one leading across a bog. Each year special events are held. In the fall, festivals called Pumpkin Palooza and Scarecrows on Display are held. In early spring, the sugar bush operation for making maple syrup can be observed and a pancake brunch is served. The arboretum is open from 8 AM to 4:30 PM during the winter months and from 8 AM to 6 PM May through October. On Sundays, the arboretum opens at 10 AM. Admission is $9 per person with children 15 and under admitted free. Yearly family memberships for $65 are available and include free admission and a reduction in class fees.

Note: Throughout the year, some free Arboretum admission days and/or times are offered. Visit the website for when these are scheduled.

Summer Children's Garden programs (952-443-1422) are offered on-site starting in May for ages kindergarten through 8th grade. The arboretum lends out garden plots to the children in the classes. All the supplies needed such as plants, seeds and tools are provided. Registration is required. Information on class fees, dates and hours along with on-line registration is available on the website. March is a good time to look into registering for these popular programs.

Children's Garden in Residence programs (952-443-1422) are offered in several urban neighborhoods. The arboretum's Plantmobile goes to these Minneapolis and St. Paul communities with a unique gardening program for children. Contact the arboretum for dates and locations. These programs are funded by grants from generous arboretum supporters.

Free Family Weekends are year-round, drop-in, hands-on family planned activity programs. For more information, call (952-443-1422) and/or check the website.

ARD GODFREY HOUSE
Richard Chute Sq.
28 University Ave. S.E. & Central Ave.
Minneapolis, 55401

612-813-5300 or 612-813-5319 (infoline)
www.ardgodfreyhouse.org

Reopened to the public in 1979, the Ard Godfrey House is Minneapolis's oldest historic remaining residence. Ard Godfrey, a millwright from Maine, built the house in 1849. He also built the first sawmill at the Falls of St. Anthony. The house was built with the first lumber sawed at the mill.

Today the house is open to the public for guided tours for visitors on Saturday and Sunday 1 PM to 4 PM in June, July and August. In groups of

10 or more, a period costumed guide shares the history of the house and Godfrey family in the tour lasting about 45 minutes. Special tours can also be arranged throughout the year with reservations by contacting the Woman's Club of Minneapolis (612-813-5300), the sponsoring organization that maintains the property owned by the Minneapolis Parks & Recreation Dept. Admission is free with donations most welcome.

Children of third grade age and up will be interested in seeing and hearing about the furnishings and toys the three Godfrey children had when they lived in the house.

Children (and others) are asked NOT to pick the dandelions, which grow on the lawn. The story is that Mrs. Godfrey had dandelion seeds sent to her from Maine so she could grow them for their edible leaves, make wine from the heads and use the roots for a beverage called "coffee." To maintain authenticity, the dandelions are protected for their historic value.

Note: Picnic tables are located on the property to use for having lunch or a snack before or after visiting the house.

*ARTSTART
ArtScraps Store
1459 St. Clair Ave.
St. Paul, 55105

651-698-2787
www.artstart.org

ArtStart can be described as an organization that provides planned activities for creating art using reusable materials, i.e., scraps. From businesses and manufacturers, the store collects their overstocks and rejects. Donations of recyclable items like buttons, fake fur, cardboard tubes, pine cones and empty pill bottles are added to the stores bins and chests of materials.

Using these materials, many that could be described as "zany", Super Scrapper classes and workshops where children can learn how to make robots, books and wacky creatures are taught by local artists and staff to children from ages 4 and older. Fees start at $10.

ArtScraps hosts birthday parties with art activity themes like Animal Shakers, Creature Masks and Fairytale Fun for ages 4 and older with fees beginning at $125.

Field trips, themed adventure weekly programs for ages 6 through 12, summer art camp experiences and special community events are all offered by this dedicated arts education non-profit organization. ArtStart's innovative programs link the arts with our environment for imaginative fun.

Call and/or visit their website and/or visit the store. Hours are Monday through Friday from 10 AM to 6 PM and Saturday from 10 AM to 4 PM.

Note: Shoppers can fill a grocery bag with materials from the bins for $5.

BACHMAN'S FLORAL & GARDEN CENTERS
6010 Lyndale Ave. S.
Minneapolis, 55419

612-861-7311
1-866-222-4626
www.bachmans.com

The flagship store on Lyndale Ave. is located on the site of the original Bachman's Garden Center. The business began in 1885 on 44 acres of farmland in Richfield. Today at their 513 acre growing site, they provide our community with a large variety of flowers, plants, trees and shrubs.

Bachman's also provides the Kids in the Garden program for children ages 3 to 10. Each class is from 10 AM to 11 PM on the first Saturday of each month year around. Because the program became so popular when first offered at the Bachman's Flagship Store on Lyndale Ave. in 2010, the classes are now also held at these additional Bachman's store locations:

Apple Valley: 7955 W. 150th St., 55124 (952-431-2242)
Eden Prairie: 770 Prairie Center Dr., 55344 (952-941-7700)
Fridley: 8200 University Ave. NE, 55432 (763-786-8200)
Maplewood: 2600 White Bear Ave., 55109 (651-770-0531)
Plymouth: 10050 6th Ave., 55441 (763-541-1188)

Each monthly class has a different theme. And it is always a hands-on activity involving plants, flowers, seeds or other nature material. Previous classes have included learning about our native birds when making a pinecone birdfeeder or the importance of composting while making a worm farm or how to care for the bulbs and winter wheat seed after planting in their creatively self-decorated garden pot. Parents are welcome to participate but not required to stay with their children, as browsing within the store is an option.

Besides the take-home creation, each child attendee receives a care sheet for plant projects, an attendance class punch card for free gift upon completing 7 classes and Garden Fun for Kids activity booklet.

Class sizes are limited to 30 at the larger Lyndale location and 10 at each of the other locations. Advance registration (612-861-7600) is required for each class. As classes fill quickly, register early. For a information on the current scheduled classes, call or check the website.

*BAKKEN LIBRARY & MUSEUM OF ELECTRICITY IN LIFE
3537 Zenith Ave. S.
W. 36 St. & W. Lake Calhoun Pkwy.
Minneapolis, 55416

612-926-3878 (infoline)
www.thebakken.org

In the late 1960s, Earl E. Bakken, co-founder of Medtronic, started collecting books, scientific instruments and other artifacts relating to the history of electricity and medicine. Today, we have the wonderful opportunity to view his collection and learn more about electricity at the Bakken Museum that is in a lovely Tudor style house located on pretty grounds near Lake Calhoun. Children age 2 and older will enjoy a visit on Super Science Saturday mornings. The Bakken is open for self-guided touring Tuesday through Saturday from 10 AM to 5 PM. Admission is $7 for adults and $5 for seniors and children 4 and older.

Note: Electricity hands-on activities for grade 1 and older are offered. These workshops are an hour long and do not require reservations. Some are scheduled for Thursday evening when the Bakken is open until 8 PM.

*BELL MUSEUM OF NATURAL HISTORY
University of Minnesota, Minneapolis Campus
10 Church St.
University Ave. & 17th Ave. S.E.
Minneapolis, 55455

612-624-7083 (infoline)
www.bellmuseum.org

This museum is a very exciting one for children. Most of the animals and birds are displayed in their natural habitat settings. The beaver exhibit is a favorite. There is even a stepstool for the very young child to use to see the inside of the beaver's lodge. Guided tours of the museum can be arranged through reservations. Family activities are held year around at the museum. Visit the website or call for a description of the current programs and events. The museum is open Tuesday through Friday from 9 AM to 5 PM, Saturdays from 10 to 5 PM and Sundays from noon to 5 PM when admission is free. Admission for the other days is $5 for adults and $3 for children ages 3 to 16 and $3 for seniors. For tours of the museum, call 612-626-9660.

Year around hands-on educational programs for preschool through grade 12 are offered by the Bell. Summer camps and some school vacation day activities are offered as well. For details on programs, costs and how to register, call (612-624-9050) or visit the website.

Note: Birthdays at the Bell are fun ways to celebrate a child's birthday.
Several options are available ranging in cost from $125 to $200 for
a party of 2 to 3 hours. Party days are Saturday and Sunday and can
include a tour, games, invitations, party bag and nature printing on
a take home T-shirt.

Located in the museum is the children's **Touch and See Room** which is
described in more detail in the T's.

*BIG STONE MINI GOLF AND SCULPTURE GARDEN
7110 Cty. Rd. 110 W.
Minnetrista, 55364

952-472-9292
www.bigstoneminigolf.com

This attraction can be a bit of a drive and challenge to find but do not give
up. Look for the big stone sign at its road entrance off 110. This is the most
unique mini-golf course one will every play.

All ages will find something of fun and of interest here. Not only is there
mini-golf but there are animals including goats, horses and Floyd, the pig,
on the grounds. One can play checkers at the huge stone table while sitting
on tree trunk benches using large gold and green metal discs. And throughout the grounds, look for the sculptures of a large turtle, giant dragonflies
and mother nature with her tree root hair as well as the mosaic chicken.

But the main attraction is the mini-golf course with each of the 13 holes a
totally separate experience. First, a warning...the serious golfer will find the
only chance for a hole-in-one is on hole No. 4, Arbor Viney. But this is not
a course for serious golf. Hole No. 1, Dead Tree Forest, consists of many
tree trunks requiring hitting and bouncing the ball around them to reach the
hole. Hole No. 7, the Holey Ship, is an upside down approximately 70 foot
long Chris Craft metal boat. On a sunny day, the colored squiggly extruded
windows cast lovely patterns in the interior mindful of stained glass.

Open from May through October, the summer hours are 10 AM to sundown
every day with reduced hours in the spring and fall months. The cost is $7
for adults and $6 for ages 8 and under. Snacks are for sale at very reasonable
prices at the Club House. And one can also feed the goats for 50 cents.

Note: Birthday parties can be held at Big Stone for a rental fee of $20.
The party location, comfortably accommodating up to 50, is at the
Stonehenge site, a circle of large stone slabs with tree stump seats.
In the center is a fire pit that can be used for roasting hot dogs...
sticks provided. Call for reservations.

BIKE MAPS
Minnesota Department of Transportation
395 John Ireland Blvd.
St. Paul, 55155

651-366-3017
www.dot.state.mn.us/bike.html

Not an attraction or activity as such but leading to many happy hours exploring are many bicycling maps. Information on Twin Cities maps, Greater Minnesota maps, State and National Maps are there. Some can even be printed for free. Others can be ordered online with costs beginning at $4.25. Their site also has important information on bicycle safety as well as links to other bicycle map websites.

The Minnesota's Book Store (651-297-3000) has biking maps for sale, too. They are located at 660 Olive St., St. Paul and are open from 8 AM to 5 PM weekdays. **www.minnesotasbookstore.com**

Note: The new State of Minnesota Bicycle Map is expected to be available in 2012. Visit the DOT website for more information on it.

*BLOOMINGTON THEATRE & ART CENTER
1800 W. Old Shakopee Rd.
Bloomington, 55431

952-563-8587
www.bloomingtonartcenter.com

Youth art classes are offered year around for ages 3 and older. Summer Art Day Camps are held from June through August for ages 3 through grade 12. Birthday parties that could include a T-shirt painting activity are popular. For all the information needed for selecting from the wide variety of programs offered, contact the center for a quarterly brochure or visit the website.

BURGER KING TOURS & BIRTHDAY PARTIES
Kids are treated like kings and queens during a tour of a Burger King restaurant. Tours may include how a new employee would be introduced to all the many steps of making a meal at Burger King special for the customer. Each child may be given a treat at the end of the tour. People of all ages are welcome but tours are scheduled only at non-rush times. Contact a nearby Burger King mornings to speak to a manager to arrange for a visit. Not all Burger King restaurants offer tours.

Note: Having a birthday party at many Burger King restaurants is possible. Some locations have Playlands. It is recommended calling up to a week in advance of the party date to let the restaurant know of your interest. The manager can then provide details and arrangements for a party at their location.

*CAFESJIAN CAROUSEL
On the Como Park Grounds
1245 Midway Pkwy.
St. Paul, 55103

651-489-4628
www.ourfaircarousel.org

In 2000, the 86-year-old carousel was relocated. The 68 handsomely restored hand-carved horses and two colorful chariots were originally built by the Philadelphia Toboggan Co. in 1914 for location on the Minnesota State Fair grounds. Today the carousel is housed in its own enclosed pavilion in Como Park west of the Como Conservatory.

Open daily from May through October, Tuesday through Sunday from 11 AM to 4 PM weekdays and 11 AM to 6 PM weekends. The 4-minute ride is $1.50 per ticket. Children under age 1 are free with a paid adult. Free parking is very close by.

Note: Rides on the carousel are free one day a month. Call or visit the website for the day.

CAPONI ART PARK AND LEARNING CENTER
1220 Diffley Rd.
Eagan, 55123

651-454-9412
www.caponiartpark.org

Family Fun Tuesdays are weekly events held at 10 AM in the park's Sculpture Garden. From the first week in June and continuing through August, a different program of approximately 1 hour entertains children along with their adult companions. The setting is outdoors on a hilly, grassy, tree shaded ground in this 60 acre art park. While sitting on blankets, picnic table benches, in strollers and the grass, attendees may be entertained by musicians, storytellers, puppeteers, dancers or theatre performances. Admission to the programs is free with a donation of $2 per person suggested.

On the day we attended, everyone was actively involved in learning about the sounds and stories of South America. On the stage under a large canopy the performers kept the audience moving, singing and even had children on stage participating by playing several of the authentic folk instruments.

For a calendar providing details on the upcoming Family Fun Tuesday programs, visit the website. It also provides information on other events held in the park including those at the Theater in the Woods.

The park grounds are open to visitors Tuesday through Sunday from May through October during the hours of 9 AM to as late as 8 PM some months. Location information and a map of the ground is also available on the web. Parking is free.

Note: Guided tours for school groups and other organizations can be arranged. The fee is $3 per person. For arrangement details, contact 651-454-9412. Self touring is possible, too. Pick up a park map in the parking lot and enjoy walking the many trails and seeing the many large sculptures. Be sure to look for the concrete snake.

*THE CHILDREN'S MUSEUM
10 W. 7th St.
St. Paul, 55102

651-225-6000 (infoline)
www.mcm.org

Upon entering the museum lobby, look for the TV screens for a guide to the day's schedule of activities and upcoming events. Then enjoy this museum built for children age 6 months to 10 years old.

There are five permanent galleries and two traveling exhibits in the museum designed to encourage children to learn through doing. The Habitot is for the youngest. Children ages 6 months to 4 years can crawl, roll and toddle through the landscapes called Forest, Prairie, Pond and Bluff Cave. The World Works gallery and other galleries are for 4 to 10 year olds. Favorites here are the thunderstorm activities. In Earth World, an anthill can be explored and clouds can be moved across the ceiling using a pulley system. Our World has a child-sized bus with moving steering wheel and buttons that turn on headlights and signal lights. The Music Studio is a popular stop with a stage and music where children can perform. The Rooftop ArtPark, designed to bring art and nature together, is located on the museum's 4th floor. Being that it is outside on the roof, it is open summer months only.

Admission is $8.95 for ages 1 to 101 years. Memberships are also available. The museum hours are 9 AM to 4 PM Tuesday through Sunday with extended hours on Friday and Saturday evenings. Closed on Monday. Parking at the World Trade Center ramp is nearby.

Note: Birthday parties can be arranged with fees beginning at $185 for non-members and $160 for members.

*THE CHILDREN'S THEATRE COMPANY (CTC)
Located in the Minneapolis Society of Fine Arts Complex
2400 3rd Ave. S.
Minneapolis, 55404

612-874-0400 or 612-874-0500 (infoline)
www.childrenstheatre.org

The Children's Theatre Company is recognized as one of the nation's best theatres for children and families. In lavish settings, it performs new plays as well as original adaptations of children's literature, folk tales and fairy tales. The plays last from one to two hours. After most matinees, discussion and demonstrations by the actors and production crew are held. Ticket prices begin at $16 and have additional service fees. Reservations are recommended.

The website has information on School Field Trips (612-872-5166) and for public group sales (612-872-5319) . Contact the theatre and/or visit the website for current productions and dates and times of performances as well as age range recommendations.

*CIRCUS JUVENTAS
1270 Montreal Ave.
St. Paul, 55116

651-699-8229
www.circusjuventas.org

Founded in 1994, this is a performing arts youth circus school for ages 3 and older. Circus skills taught to the very young begin with acrobatics, juggling and creative movement. Classes are held Monday through Saturdays with fees beginning at $160.

Their spectacular celebratory big shows are held at the Circus Juventas Big Top in the spring and summer. The performances combines storytelling with aerial stunts and acrobatics in the tradition of the famous touring Cirque du Soleil troupe. Ticket prices begin at $12.50. Discounts are available for groups of 25 or more.

COMO PARK'S MARJORIE MCNEELY CONSERVATORY
Midway Pkwy. & Kaufman Dr.
St. Paul, 55103

651-487-8201 or 651-487-8200 (infoline)
www.comozooconservatory.org

The conservatory is open 365 days of the year with hours from 10 AM to 4 PM during the winter months and 10 AM to 6 PM the rest of the year.

There are five main rooms, the palm dome, the sunken gardens, the fern room, the bonsai display and the North Wing for the tropical fruit and flowering plants. Children especially enjoy the sight of grapefruit and oranges growing on the trees in the tropical room and the large goldfish swimming in the sunken garden ponds. Admission is free. Suggested donations of $2 for adults and $1 for children are greatly appreciated.

Spectacular seasonal flower displays in the sunken gardens are a must to see. The poinsettias during the winter holidays and the tulips and other flowering bulbs during the springtime are especially cheerful. Bring the camera.

Note: **Como Ordway Memorial Japanese Garden** can be visited beginning early in May and continuing into September. The Annual Lantern Lighting Festival is held on a Sunday in August. During the lantern lighting ceremony, six stone lanterns and floating paper lanterns are lit.

COMO PARK ZOO
1225 Estabrook Dr.
St. Paul, 55103

651-487-8201 or 651-487-8200 (infoline)
www.comozooconservatory.org/zoo

A favorite of our family all year round. During the winter months the zoo grounds and buildings are open from 10 AM to 4 PM. During the summer months the zoo grounds and buildings are open from 10 AM to 6 PM.

There are many animals for children to see including Sparky, the sea lion, who performs several times daily during the summer in the Aquatic Building, the gorillas in the Primate Building and the giraffes in the African Hoofed Stock exhibit.

The Visitor's Center is the primary entrance to the Zoo and Conservatory. Located between the Conservatory and the carousel, it is staffed during building hours of 10 AM to 4 PM winter months and 10 AM to 6 PM summer months.

The Education Department (651-487-8272) is the contact point for classes, group tours, field trips and other programs and activities. Call between 8 AM and 4 PM to talk to the staff or leave a message.

Note: Birthday parties can be held at the Zoo. Choose from 6 different themes. The party arrangements include games and educational activities. Costs begin at $185 and are limited to 15 guests. Visit the zoo's website for additional information and/or call the Education Department.

*COMO TOWN AMUSEMENT PARK
Midway Pkwy.
St. Paul, 55103

651-487-2121
www.comotown.com

Located adjacent to the Zoo, all the rides at this child-centered amusement park have been selected for children ages 1 to 12. Many of the rides allow children to participate in some way. There is the Tilt-A-Whirl, the Traffic Jam! Bumper Cars and the Fire Brigade among others. On the Fire Brigade, a child can actually spray water at a pretend fire. Rides are "pay as you play". Rides range from 4 to 18 points per ride. Points are 23 cents each. Daily wrist bands for unlimited rides are available for purchase. Como Town has food stands and carts, planned activities like face painting and a birthday party area.

The main entrance to the amusement park is near the stoplight on Midway Parkway. The nearest parking is in the Wolf Lot. The fenced-in area is open for rides daily from 10 AM to as late as 9 PM some days during the summer. After Labor Day, it is open weekends from 10 AM to 6 PM through October. Check the website or call to avoid disappointments.

NOTES

*DODGE NATURE CENTER
365 W. Marie Ave.
West St. Paul, 55118

651-455-4531
www.dodgenaturecenter.org

The Thomas Irvine Dodge Nature Center is open to school and other organized groups from 8 AM to 4:30 PM Monday through Friday. The center is open to families and individuals through attendance in public programs and classes held evenings and from 10 AM to 4 PM Saturdays. Class fees are from $7 and up with members receiving a discount.

The center's grounds are open to the public from sunup to sundown everyday for hiking their six miles of trails. If hiking during business hours, sign in at the Main Office on Marie Ave.

The emphasis of the center is on providing special nature study activities for students and others. There are 320 acres of mixed woods and grassland for supervised study, nature hiking and snowshoeing. On the grounds are a red barn converted into a schoolhouse for classroom studies and another barn remodeled into a museum on the upper level and a lab on the lower. The lab contains glass tanks with live turtles and snakes and frogs. A short hike away a large model farm shows typical farm crops and animals. A naturalist plans with the group beforehand the activities for study during the visit. Some topics to choose may include seeds, insects, wild edible plants, habitats, pond life, weather station, study of bees, model farm, fall orchard and orienteering. During the summer, the center offers family gardening programs and Summer Under the Sun Camp for children. Contact the center for a brochure or visit their website for descriptions of all their class offerings. Contact them also for arrangements for a school or group weekday nature study program.

Note: Special events are held throughout the year. Family Farm Festival in the spring, Halloween Extravaganza in the fall and Frosty Fun in the winter are very popular ones. Visit the website or call for dates and details.

*EDINA ART CENTER
4701 W. 64th St.
Edina, 55435

952-903-5780
www.edinaartcenter.com

Young people's classes for infants and up are taught at the center weekdays and Saturdays. There are also special Sunday art events and programs.

Children can explore the arts through classes and workshops in painting, drawing, pottery, jewelry, music, media arts and family art. Some are free. Others start at $11 with grants available to supplement the fees. Members have a reduced fee. Visit their website or call for a brochure listing all their activities as well as membership information. The center is open Monday through Friday and Saturday mornings.

Note: Summer Art Camps are held mornings and afternoons June through August. Tuition starts at $69. Call in March or visit their website for registration information and a listing of the camps offered. Some past camps have included activities of modeling clay dinosaurs, maskmaking and creating jewelry.

*EDINBOROUGH PARK IN EDINA
7700 York Ave. S.
Edina, 55435

952-833-9540 (infoline)
www.edinboroughpark.com

This is an indoor park that is a good alternative during bad weather. Within the Playpark are Adventure Peak, the Great Hall and the Tot Area. Don't forget socks. They are required in Playpark's Adventure Peak area. Even moms and dads need them here. Shoes are required for all the other areas.

The Playpark is open from 9 AM to 9 PM Monday through Saturday and Sunday from 9 AM to 6 PM. Daily fee is $6 per child and free for adults with child's paid admission. An additional fee of $6 per person is charged for swimming. Call in advance or check the website for open swim times.

Note: Adventure Peak Birthday Party packages are available beginning at $80. Ask Angie for the details (952-833-9540).

ELOISE BUTLER WILD FLOWER GARDEN & BIRD SANCTUARY
Theodore Wirth Park
1339 Theodore Wirth Pkwy.
Between Interstate 394 and Glenwood Ave.
Minneapolis, 55411

612-370-4903 (infoline)
www.minneapolisparks.com

Located in Theodore Wirth Park, this is a delightful garden containing a marshy bog, a wooded glen and upland prairie as well as a bird refuge. Hiking through the sanctuary and gardens on a crisp fall or early spring day when the buds are just appearing or anytime, really, is an enjoyable experience for all. Open from April through mid-October, 7:30 AM to one hour before sunset, this is a favorite walking spot for many Twin City families. Weekend programs and public tours are available, too. Call or visit the website (Gardens & Historical Sites) for information on dates and times.

*EXCELSIOR STREETCAR LINE
Minnesota Streetcar Museum (MSM)
3rd & George Streets
Excelsior, 55331

952-992-1096
www.trolleyride.org

From early May into November weather permitting, passengers can board the streetcar that departs from the Linden Hills Station and Lake Calhoun Platform. The ride is about 15 minutes long and may have a brief stop at the carbarn to look at streetcar restoration in progress. The streetcars depart every fifteen minutes daily with operational hours varying with the day of the week. Tickets are $2 per person. Children 3 and under ride free. Charters are also available with at least a 2 week advance reservation requested. Visit the website for additional details and a location map.

*FARMERS' MARKET OF ST. PAUL
290 E. 5th St.
St. Paul, 55101

651-227-8101 or 651-227-6856 (infoline)
www.stpaulfarmersmarket.com

Historically, the St. Paul Farmers Market has existed since 1854. In the spring of 1982 the St. Paul Farmers' Market opened in downtown St. Paul at 5th and Wall Streets. For sale are fresh, locally grown vegetables, fruits, flowers and products like honey and cheese. The season runs from late April through November. The market sponsors special events and activities during the season. On many weekends there is live music.

Today, in season, the main downtown market is open Friday afternoons and weekend mornings. It is open Saturday mornings the remainder of the year. In addition, there are 18 satellite locations. The satellites are in church, shopping center and other parking lot locations in the St. Paul and surrounding area. In season, each satellite is open one day a week. Call the infoline or visit the website for their locations and the current garden produce for sale.

FIRE STATIONS

Children always seem to enjoy a visit to the fire station. Most fire stations welcome them if the visit is scheduled in advance. The fire engines, the alarm system and the living quarters are shown and explained at most visits. The fire fighters like to emphasize fire prevention in the home and encourage children to ask questions about their work. The best tours are those which are closest to where children live or go to school; so contact your nearest fire station to inquire about a visit.

*FIREFIGHTERS HALL & MUSEUM
664 22nd Ave. N.E.
Minneapolis, 55418

612-623-3817
www.firehallmuseum.org

The firefighters collection, after 4 moves in 15 years, finally found a permanent home with funding help from the late Capt. Bill Daniels and his wife Bonnie. The museum is in a large brick building with lots of space to display their fire fighting apparatus. The most modern is a 1984 fire truck. The oldest piece is an 1860's hand pump fire truck. Children with supervision can climb on a fire truck, operate the hand fire pump, dress as a firefighter with boots, helmet and turnout coat. One of the most popular activities is the real Tiller cab with video simulator…so popular, that a second cab has been added. The newest addition is a firefighter's sliding pole…see a picture of it on the website.

School field trips and other groups should be sure to schedule a time for a safety talk in the education room. Especially meaningful is the fire and smoke demonstration using the Graco Corporation's funded scale model house with cut-off front.

The museum is also a great location for arranging a birthday party. The cost is $25 in addition to the admission fee.

The museum is open 9 AM to 4 PM Saturday and weekdays for groups of 10 or more by appointment. Admission is $6 for adults, $5 for seniors and $3 for children 3 to 12. This includes a fire engine ride on Saturdays through the nearby area April through October weather permitting. Parking is conveniently located next to the museum.

Bring your camera!

Note: The Minneapolis Police Department's exhibit room with its memorabilia includes a display case of unique confiscated weapons, posters, uniform items and an officers' commemorative wall.

*FORT SNELLING
Minnesota Historical Society (MHS)
200 Tower Ave.
Accessible from State Hwys. 5 & 55 or Interstate Hwy. 494
St. Paul, 55111

612-726-1171
www.mnhs.org/places/sites/hfs

Historic Fort Snelling was built in the early 1820s. Its presence was needed to maintain peace between the Ojibway and Dakota Indians, to protect the American fur traders from the British and to exert U.S. military influence in this area. Today, it is one of our most interesting and well-preserved historic landmarks. Children will enjoy seeing the Round Tower that was once a lookout, the Guardhouse and jail cells, the blacksmith and sutler's shops, the Schoolhouse, barracks and hospital.

The fort is open Monday through Saturday from 10 AM to 5 PM and Sunday from noon to 5 PM Memorial Day weekend through Labor Day. Staffed with costumed guides, visitors are encouraged to take part in the everyday life at the fort. This might include stitching on a quilt, shouldering a musket and singing along with the soldiers. Special events during a day's visit might include seeing a guard inspection, a retreat ceremony and a cannon demonstration.

Admission is $10 for adults, $8 for senior citizens, $5 for children age 6 through 17 and free for children age 5 and under. Educational groups are required to make reservations in writing or by calling. The reduced fee for educational groups is $5 per person and requires a group size minimum of 10.

Note: The Fort Snelling Museum Store & History Center located on the grounds of the fort is open the same days and hours as the fort. However, calling September through May, one may find the center staffed and open. In addition to the exhibits and gift shop, a 17-minute film showing the history of the fort can be viewed here. No admission is charged for visiting the center at any time.

*FORT SNELLING STATE PARK
101 Snelling Lake Rd. at State Hwy. 5 & Post Rd.
St. Paul, 55111

612-725-2389 or 612-725-2724
www.dnr.state.mn.us

Located near Fort Snelling on Snelling Lake Road is this wonderful urban state park. Picnic tables, a swimming beach, Thomas C. Savage Visitor

Center and cross-country skiing are here for the enjoyment of visitors. Admission is $5 per vehicle for a daily pass. An annual pass for all Minnesota State Park admittance is $25. The park is open from 8 AM to 10 PM. The Visitor Center (612-725-2724) is open from 8 AM to 4 PM and is described in more detail in the T's.

*FOSHAY TOWER OBSERVATION DECK
W Hotel
821 Marquette Ave.
Minneapolis, 55402

612-215-3783

The observation deck is located on the top of the Foshay Tower on the 32nd floor. This is one of the best observation decks in the Twin Cities. It is an open deck with a surrounding wall topped by metal bars for safety. It is now open year around. The days and hours when open are Monday through Saturday from noon to 9 PM. Admission is $8 for adults and $5 for students and seniors. Children 12 and under are free.

Note: Modeled after the Washington Monument, the tower was built in 1929 for $25 million dollars. A small museum showing the history of the tower and its first owner, Wilbur B. Foshay, can be visited on the 30th floor.

*FOSSIL HUNTING
Twin City Brickyards below Cherokee Park
Lillydale, 55107

651-632-5111
www.stpaul.gov

Two miles southwest of downtown St. Paul in Lilydale Regional Park on the banks of the Mississippi River seashells can be found. Over 550 million years ago most of Minnesota was covered by a shallow, warm sea. In that sea lived coral, snails, crinoids, clams and other species of small water life.

Today, an authorization permit is necessary for exploring these geological fossils which are located on the former site of the Twin City Brickyards quarry. The preserve area is under the management of the City of St. Paul's Division of Parks & Recreation from whom authorization is required. The Lilydale Fossil Hunting Permit is available on their website...search on Lilydale and select Permit. Or obtain a permit form by calling the Park Permit Office at 651-632-5111 between 7 AM and 3:30 PM Monday through Friday. The permit fee is $10 or $25 depending on the size of the group. Permits are issued beginning February 1 for dates between April 1 and October 31.

FRANCONIA SCULPTURE PARK
29836 St. Croix Trial
Intersection of Hwy. 8 & Hwy. 95
Franconia, 55074

651-257-6668
www.franconia.org

Newly discovered and ready for exploring is this 20-acre park in Chisago County…a 45 minute drive from the Twin Cities. It is free and open to the public 365 days a year from dawn to dusk. The Information Center is open 8:30 AM to 5 PM weekdays. Pickup here a flyer for self guided touring. Free guided tours are offered Sundays May through October at 2 PM.

Fun art education opportunities for children include Saturday hands-on sculpture workshops in June and July for ages 4 and up. The fee is $25 per class. Special events are held throughout the year. There is the Arbour Day program in April with tree planting and the Summer Solstice in June. The Annual Arts & Artist celebration is held in September when the installation of new sculptures occurs and a parking fee of $5 is charged.

The website includes park details. Its grounds are very accessible. It has over 70 sculptures…many of which can be climbed upon. It has guided tours for school and other organized groups with advanced reservations. And it has online art activities.

GAMMELGÅRDEN MUSEUM
20880 Olinda Trail N.
PO Box 67
Scandia, 55073

651-433-5033
www.gammelgardenmuseum.org

This newly discovered and explored museum is found to be devoted to portraying and preserving Swedish immigrant heritage. Gammelgården is Swedish for Old Farm. The Immigrant Hus, the 1850's built immigrant house, and the Ladugard, the barn built in 1868, are both representative of old Swedish farm structures. They are located on the site of the first Swedish settlement in Minnesota. Other buildings on the 11 acres are the first parsonage of Elim Lutheran Church, built in 1868, a typical 1850s Swedish vacation cottage and the Välkommen Hus welcome house.

We toured and explored during the Scandia Spelmansstamma, an annual Swedish music celebration held the third Saturday in August. Besides the performances by the fiddlers and dancers, we found the building tours most interesting. The traditionally dressed guides in each talked about customs and living conditions of the times. We learned that women slept in the house loft and were seated on the left side of the church. And we were told that the church built in 1856 was Elim's first and was then sold to a farmer for storing hay. Children's activities that day included playing the game "stick & hoop" and others of the mid-1850"s. Admission and tours are free.

The museum has other annual events and offers tours and children's programs and field trips. Public tours are Friday through Sunday on the hour from 1 PM to 3 PM May to mid-October. Cost is $5 for adults and free for children under 12. Tours and field trips for children at other times can be arranged by calling 651-464-1329.

Located on County Road 3 across from Elim Lutheran Church in Scandia, the museum is about an hours drive from the Twin Cities. Call or visit the website for current visitor information including schedule of events and directions.

Note: The Comin' to Amerika program is for children kindergarten age through grade 6. Through attendance at the two-day-long program, children experience what it is like to be an immigrant in the 1800's. The programs are offered in July and August. The cost is $25 per child. Pre-registration is required. The details including photos from previous programs are on the website or call 651-464-4922 for information.

*GIBBS MUSEUM
Of Pioneer and Dakotah Life
2097 W. Larpenteur Ave.
Falcon Heights, 55113

651-646-8629
www.rchs.com/gbbsfm2.htm

Farm life in the period of 1900-1910 is portrayed in the buildings housing this museum. The Gibbs family farmhouse built from 1854 to 1874 can be toured along with the one-room schoolhouse built in 1878 and the white barn which houses farm animals. Also on the grounds are a large red barn, a Dakota tipi and bark lodge and a sod house that was Heman and Jane Gibbs first home. Events are held on weekends and at holiday times. Events have included a country festival with old-time activities, an old-time Halloween of the 1800's and Dakota Day with traditional Dakota Indian activities, crafts and food. Owned and operated by the Ramsey County Historical Society (RCHS), the museum is open May through mid-November on Tuesdays through Sundays from noon to 4 PM. Admission is $8 adults, $7 for seniors and $5 for ages 2 to 16. For a few special seasonal events, admission is higher. RCHS members are free. Group tour rates are available with reservations required. For a current listing of activities held at Gibbs, call RCHS or select the link to Calendar of Events on the website.

A number of different Summer Day Camps for Children ages 4 through 11 are offered. On each Friday in July, Summer Schoolhouse, a one-day program is held in the one-room schoolhouse for children grades 2 through 6. Class is from 9 AM to 1 PM. Tuition is $39 per child. Another, Pioneer PeeWees, is Wednesday mornings in August for children ages 4 through 6. It is from 9 AM to 11 AM. Tuition is $19 per child. The programs includes all materials, a snack and drink. Reservations are required. To enroll call or mail in the online printable registration form.

GOVERNOR'S RESIDENCE TOUR
Home of the Governor of the State of Minnesota
1006 Summit Ave.
St. Paul, 55105

651-297-2161 (infoline)
www.admin.state.mn.us/govres

From June through August, on the first, second and third Tuesday, summer touring is normally possible. The self-guided, open-house tour includes the main floor and gardens where the Children's Garden is located. Changing exhibits of Minnesota artists' work are showcased in many of the rooms.

On the lower level, one room is devoted to photographs of former First Minnesota first ladies. The tour will be of most interest to children of age 6 and older. Photo ID is required for entry.

Note: Open Houses are held in early to mid-December during the holidays some years. Also Halloween has been celebrated at the residence with treats given to children in costume who stop by with an adult.

*GREAT CLIPS IMAX THEATRE
At The Minnesota Zoo
12000 Zoo Blvd.
Apple Valley, 55124

952-431-4629 (infoline)
1-877-660-IMAX
www.imax.com/minnesota

Conveniently located next to the Zoo entrance, the IMAX usually has several shows/experiences to choose from daily. Happy Feet II: an IMAX 3D Experience and Under the Sea 3D are a couple of the past shows. Call or visit the website for the current selections and coming soon offerings. Ticket prices are $7 to $12 for seniors and children 12 and under and $9.50 to $16 for adults 13 to 64. Reduced ticket prices can be arranged for bookings of public groups of 20 or more and for educational programs by calling 952-997-9714 or 1-877-660-4629.

GREAT HARVEST BREAD CO.
www.stpaulbread.com

Bonnie's Neighborhood Bread Business, 534 Selby Ave.,
**   St. Paul, 55102 (651-221-1057)**
Woodbury, Lightfaire Center in Tamarack Village,
**   Woodbury, 55125 (651-578-9756)**
Burnsville, 1100 E. Co. Rd. 42,
**   Burnsville, 55337 (952-891-4767)**
Michael & Ruth's Minnetonka Bread Store, 17416 Minnetonka Blvd.,
**   Minnetonka, 55345 (952-476-2515)**
Tom & Sally's Family Owned Bread Store, 4314 Upton Ave. S.,
**   Minneapolis, 55410 (612-929-2899)**

Tuesday and Wednesday mornings throughout the year, tour groups for children of preschool age and up are invited to a behind-the-scenes look at bread making. This includes the operations of milling and of dough processing and a look at all the other machines used to make their delicious bread and really big healthy cookies. To reserve a time, call during store hours that for most stores are 6:30 AM to 6:30 PM Monday through Friday and 6:30 AM to 5 PM Saturdays.

*GREATER TWIN CITIES' YOUTH SYMPHONIES (GTCYS)
528 Hennepin Ave. Suite 404
Minneapolis, 55403

612-870-7611
www.gtcys.org

Founded in 1972, GTCYS is the largest youth symphony program in the country with over 500 musicians in their 6 orchestras which are the Symphony, Philharmonic, Sinfonia, Philharmonia, Concertino and Concert. They perform many concerts during their annual September through May season. The performances are held throughout the Twin Cities area including at Orchestra Hall as well as churches, retirement homes and schools. Many concerts are free. However, some have a small admission fee. GTCYS have been invited to tour and perform in many U.S. cities and international locations including Fiji, Japan, England and China.

Auditions to become a member of one of the many symphonies are held each spring in May or June and in December. Talented young musicians of all ages and abilities through grade 12 can try out by scheduling an audition appointment. There is a $35 audition registration fee. Tuition for membership in one of the orchestras ranges from $545 to $640 a year. For more information including applying for scholarships, call the GTCYS office or visit their website.

Young people playing for other young people and adults; what could be more inspiring and special!

Note: GTCYS also has a summer orchestra program. Two orchestras form and each meets to practice once a week in June and July. The final session is a concert for all. Tuition is $210 with a $20 registration fee. Call and/or visit the website for information on scholarship availability and application forms.

*GUTHRIE THEATER TOURS & CLASSES
818 2nd St. S.
Minneapolis, 55415

612-377-2224
www.guthrietheater.org

The tours, classes and programs offered by the Guthrie are a way to reach out to children in the area and provide them with experiences in theater crafts and arts. One, The Backstage Tour, suggested for children of upper elementary ages and older, takes them to the backstage area, underworld, costume shop and dressing rooms. Groups are told about the history of the theater and are given an explanation about its work-a-day life.

Scheduled tours are Friday, Saturday and Sunday mornings at 10 AM with reservations (612-377-2224) needed in advance. Tickets are $10 for adults and $6 for students and seniors. Visit the website or call the Guthrie Ticket Office 612-377-2224 for additional information. Group tours for 20 or more attendees at other times can be arranged by calling 612-225-6240 (infoline).

Note: Once a year a Free Family Open House is held on a Sunday afternoon. Visitors can watch a rehearsal, try on costumes, play theater games and see how the stage props are built. One may even be able to try your hand at making a theatre mask. Check the website for an announcement of the current year's date.

*HARRIET ALEXANDER NATURE CENTER (HANC)
Roseville Parks & Recreation Dept.
2520 N. Dale St.
Roseville, 55113

651-765-4262
www.ci.roseville.mn.us/parks

The Harriet Alexander Nature Center is located in Roseville's Central Park. The nature area has 52 acres of marsh, prairie and forest habitats. Nature programs about everything from bug talk to night sky are offered here. School groups, families, day care centers, seniors, scout troops, bird clubs and anyone else interested should contact the center and make the necessary reservations to attend the special programs. Fees for programs begin at $4 to $6 per person and up.

Information on current programs and fees can be received by contacting the center or visiting the website. The importance of environmental awareness through studying nature is stressed in all their programs. Pre-registration at 651-792-7110 is required for all special programs.

Special events are held throughout the year including natural egg dying in the spring, the Wild Rice Fall Festival and an Open House in the winter. Details, see the website.

The centers hours of operation are Tuesday through Saturday from 10 AM to 4 PM and Sunday from 1 PM to 4 PM.

HARRIET ISLAND REGIONAL PARK
City of St. Paul, Div. of Parks & Recreation
50 Harriet Island
St. Paul, 55107

651-292-7010
http://www.ci.stpaul.mn.us/index.aspx

This 100 year old renovated park located along the bank of the Mississippi River between Wabasha St. Bridge and the High Bridge has a tot-lot playground, the Harriet Bishop Playground. Harriet Bishop was Minnesota's first public school teacher. A new addition to the park is the Adventure Playground, a play area with forms created to look like driftwood and mussel shells.

Take the Great River Stairs to the river's edge and Riverwalk. The Walk, built of steppingstones, allowed groups and individuals to have a message inscribed into a stone for a $125 donation. These messages are fun to read. One stone says simple "We Love the River." To locate park information on the website, select the Government option and under Parks & Recreation find Harriet Island.

*IN THE HEART OF THE BEAST PUPPET & MASK THEATRE (HOBT)
1500 E. Lake St.
Minneapolis, 55407

612-721-2535
www.hobt.org

From October through March, families can attend Saturday morning Puppet Shows for Kids in this most colorful and unique building. The puppet stage and viewing area is set up in the Avalon Theater lobby for the 10 AM show repeated again at noon. Children sit on the large red carpet near the stage while adults sit on chairs behind them. Sitting is limited and no reservations are necessary. Donations of $2 or $4 are requested.

There are over 20 different shows every season. Each show is about 45 minutes. The puppeteers maybe in costume and visible. There is often live music accompanying the show. It is evident that all ages enjoy the show as the cheering, clapping, sighing and laughing continue throughout the performance. At the end of the show, children are invited to look at the puppets and to ask questions. Also after the 10 AM show, a puppet workshop called "Make-n-Take" based on the day's show theme is offered in their classroom. This is a family activity with a fee of $5 per individual. Advance registration is recommended but can be made at the 10 AM show.

For upcoming show announcements, visit the website or pickup up a current flyer at the theatre.

HENNEPIN COUNTY PUBLIC LIBRARY (HCPL)
12601 Ridgedale Dr.
Minnetonka, 55305

952-847-5669 or 952-847-KNOW
www.hclib.org

Children are very important users of libraries. A child may have a library card at any age when applied for accompanied by an adult. Children's books, magazines, CDs and DVDs can be checked-out for 1 to 3 weeks. There is a fine for overdue children's checked out materials. Most of the libraries offer weekly storytimes for children of preschool and kindergarten ages. Many libraries have children's year around events and all have summer reading programs. Some of the librarians go to schools to talk to children about the library. As the hours vary from library to library, check with the library near you before going.

AUGSBURG PARK: 7100 Nicollet Ave., Richfield, 55423 (612-543-6200)

BROOKDALE: 6125 Shingle Creek Pkwy.,
Brooklyn Center, 55430 (612-543-5600)

BROOKLYN PARK: 8600 Zane Ave. N., 55443 (612-543-6225)

CHAMPLIN: 12154 Ensign Ave. N., 55316 (612-543-6250)

EAST LAKE: 2727 E. Lake St., Minneapolis, 55406, (612-543-8425)

EDEN PRAIRIE: 565 Eden Prairie Ctr. Dr., 55344 (612-543-6275)

EDINA: 5280 Grandview Sq., 55436 (612-543-6325)

EXCELSIOR: 343 3rd St., 55331 (612-543-6350)

FRANKLIN: 1314 E. Franklin Ave., Mpls, 55404 (612-543-6925)

GOLDEN VALLEY: 830 Winnetka Ave. N., 55427 (612-543-6375)

HOPKINS: 22 11th Ave. N., 55343 (612-543-6400)

HOSMER: 347 E. 36th St., Minneapolis, 55408 (612-543-6900)

LINDEN HILLS: 2900 W. 43rd St., Minneapolis, 55410 (612-543-6825)

LONG LAKE: 1865 Wayzata Blvd. W., 55356 (612-543-6425)

MAPLE GROVE: 8001 Main St. N., 55369, (612-543-6450)

MAPLE PLAIN: 5184 Main St. E., 55359 (612-543-5700)

MINNEAPOLIS CENTRAL: 300 Nicollet Mall, 55401 (612-543-8000)

Note: The Minneapolis Central Children's Library (952-847-8047) has an extensive language collection of children's books. There are many books in over 30 different languages including Vietnamese,

Chinese, Somali, Oromo (East Africa), Hmong, Hindi, Russian and an especially large collection in Spanish. Many of these are picture books. It should also be noted the Children's Library has a collection of Braille books with English text.

MINNETONKA: 17524 Excelsior Blvd., 55345 (612-543-5725)

NOKOMIS: 5100 34th Ave. S., Minneapolis, 55417 (612-543-6800)

NORTH REGIONAL: 1315 Lowry Ave. N., Mpls, 55411 (612-543-8450)

NORTHEAST: 2200 Central Ave. N.E., Mpls, 55418 (612-543-6775)

OSSEO: 415 Central Ave., 55369 (612-543-5750)

OXBORO: 8801 Portland Ave. S., Bloomington, 55420 (612-543-5775)

PENN LAKE: 8800 Penn Ave. S., Bloomington, 55431 (612-543-5800)

PIERRE BOTTINEAU: 55 Broadway St. N.E., Mpls, 55413 (612-543-6850)

PLYMOUTH: 15700 36th Ave. N., 55446 (612-543-5825)

RIDGEDALE: 12601 Ridgedale Dr., Minnetonka, 55305 (612-543-8800)

ROCKFORD ROAD: 6401 42nd Ave. N., Crystal, 55427 (612-543-5875)

ROGERS: 21300 John Milless Dr., 55374 (612-543-6050)

ROOSEVELT: 4026 28th Ave. S., Minneapolis, 55406 (612-543-6700)

ST. ANTHONY: 2941 Pentagon Dr. N.E., 55418 (612-543-6075)

ST. BONIFACIUS: 8624 Kennedy Memorial Dr., 55375 (612-543-6100)

ST. LOUIS PARK: 3240 Library Lane, 55426 (612-543-6125)

SOUTHDALE: 7001 York Ave. S., Edina, 55435 (612-543-5900)

SOUTHEAST: 1222 SE 4th St., Minneapolis, 55414 (612-543-6725)

SUMNER: 611 Van White Memorial Blvd., Mpls, 55411 (612-543-6875)

WALKER: 2880 Hennepin Ave., Minneapolis, 55408 (612-543-8400)

WASHBURN: 5244 Lyndale Ave. S., Mpls, 55419 (612-543-8375)

WAYZATA: 620 Rice St., 55391 (612-543-6150)

WEBBER PARK: 4310 Webber Pkwy., Mpls, 55412 (612-543-6750)

WESTONKA: 2079 Commerce Blvd., Mound, 55364 (612-543-6175)

Note: Childish Films, a program series of short children's movies, are shown at the Minneapolis Central Library, Pohlad Hall, on the third Saturday of the month at 10:30 AM. Families with pre-school age children of 3 and older will enjoy these films specially selected for a younger audience. The Red Balloon and Sleeping Beauty have been shown at previous programs. Each event includes a pre-show activity. Repeat performance are held at the Southdale library in the winter and the Brookdale library in the spring. For current information on the up-coming films, on the website **www.supporthclib. org** select Events for the listing Childish Films.

*HENNEPIN HISTORY MUSEUM
2303 3rd Ave. S.
Minneapolis, 55404

612-870-1329
www.hennepinhistory.org

The museum is housed in an old mansion. Its exhibits change throughout the years but always reflect local history from historic toys to technology. Look for these that show and tell about growing up in Hennepin County and include hands-on activities for children and adults to do together.

The museum has an especially fine collection of North American Indian artifacts and beadwork that is occasionally on display. The Century of the Child is a permanent exhibit. The museum is open Tuesday 10 AM to 2 PM and Wednesday through Sunday from 1 to 5 PM. Admission is $5 for adults and $1 for students under 18 and seniors.

HIGHPOINT PRINTMAKING CENTER
912 E. Lake St.
Minneapolis, 55408

612-871-1326
www.highpointprintmaking.org

Free Ink Days are held four Saturday afternoons a year from 1 PM to 5 PM. Recommended for children ages 7 or older and accompanied by an adult, hands-on printmaking activities make for a creative fun time. Call or check on their website for an announcement of the next.

Staff will plan printmaking activities for groups of children ages 7 or older to be held at their center. And they will also work with teachers to plan an activity at the center that ties into an area of classroom study. Contact the center for making these arrangements.

*HISTORY THEATRE
30 E. 10th St.
St. Paul, 55101

651-292-4323 (infoline)
www.historytheatre.com

This theatre performs plays that bring to life events that helped shape Minnesota and Midwestern history. Authentic music, costumes and original scripts are used. The website has information on the current season's schedule of plays.

Performance times are Thursday, Friday and Saturday at 7:30 PM with a Sunday matinee at 2 PM. Matinee performances are also available at other times with advance arrangements. Tickets are $25 to $32. Discounts for adult, senior and student groups of 12 of more can be arranged by calling 651-292-4320.

INDIAN MOUNDS PARK
Dayton's Bluff
10 Mounds Blvd.
At Earl St. & Mounds Blvd.
St. Paul, 55106

651-632-5111
www.stpaul.gov/facilities.aspx

The park has historical interest in that it is believed to have been a memorial site for local Native American Indian tribes. These burial mounds, sacred for over 2,000 years, deserve our respectful care.

The park also offers a spectacular view of the river below and the St. Paul municipal airport south of the city. The park has a tot lot with swings and slides. Nearby are picnic tables and benches.

INSECT COLLECTION
University of Minnesota, St. Paul Campus
Dept. of Entomology
219 Hodson Hall
1980 Follwell Ave.
St. Paul, 55108

612-624-1254
www.entomology.umn.edu/museum

Located on the fourth floor of Hodson Hall is an insect exhibit in display cases and a new, permanent exhibit, The Art of Entomology. On the third floor, an insect museum with current holdings at time of a recent visit recorded as 3,565,200 specimens representing 48,416 species. For the most recent count, check their website. Call at least 1 week in advance to arrange a tour. A reservation is required for visits to the Insect Collection. A group of 6 to 12 members is preferred. All ages are welcome but the tour is more suited for ages 6 and older. The fourth floor exhibits can be viewed during the building hours weekdays and Saturday afternoons. Insects big and small from all over the world are identified in this very unique collection.

NOTES

*JACKSON STREET ROUNDHOUSE
Minnesota Transportation Museum (MTM)
193 E. Pennsylvania Ave.
St. Paul, 55101

651-228-0263
www.trainride.org

Our community is fortunate to have one of the first railroad maintenance shops in Minnesota restored and open to the public. This is a train museum for children and adults. Immediately upon entering, the Red Cedar & Western #2 steam locomotive with coal car draws attention. A current restoration project that will actually operate when completed has a sign that reads "Please do not climb on me. I don't want anyone to get hurt." However, most small children cannot resist a quick climb on before getting caught. By diverting their attention to the ramp leading to the many restored railcars and locomotives on the second level, all visitors will find this continually growing museum staffed by enthusiastic volunteers, an attraction to explore again and again.

Look for and read about the 1893 Drover's Coach, the Hustle Muscle, the 1890 Gopher Business Car and the Dan Patch. Take a break and watch the children build a Thomas the Tank railroad line with engines and cars on the wooden tracked tables in the children's play area. Call to arrange field trips for schools and other groups.

With volunteer staff permission on Saturdays and other times by appointment, children of all ages and most adults should find interesting watching the volunteers work on the diesel and steam engines in the Restoration Shop.

The roundhouse is open Wednesday 10 AM to 4 PM when admission is $5 for ages 2 to 4, $6 students ages 5 to 15, seniors $6 and adults $7. On Saturday it is open from 10 AM to 5 PM when the admission fee $5 for ages 2 to 4, $8 for students, $8 for seniors and $10 for adults and includes a ride on the train or caboose or the newly added classic bus. The rides are only available on Saturday. The passenger car, our favorite, is pulled by a locomotive that authentically whistles as it starts down the track. The trips are about 12 to 15 minutes.

Note: A birthday can be celebrated at the museum. Fees begin at $100 for two hours use of the private party railcar in addition to the admission per person fee. It should also be noted that other groups can make arrangements to come at other times through calling for this information.

*JAMES J. HILL HOUSE

Minnesota Historical Society (MHS)
240 Summit Ave.
St. Paul, 55102

651-297-2555
www.mnhs.org/places/sites/jjhh/index.html

This is the home of the builder of the Great Northern Railroad, James J. Hill. It was completed in 1891 at a cost of over $931,000. The home has 42 rooms, 13 bathrooms, 22 fireplaces and a very large 100-foot reception hall. Programs and tours are held regularly throughout the year. There have been lectures on its architecture, parlor concerts, a 150th Birthday party celebration in 1988 and a play about how the Hill House servants prepared for the holidays.

The house is open for guided public tours every 30 minutes Wednesday through Saturday from 10 AM to 3:30 PM and Sunday 1 to 3:30 PM. Advance reservations are recommended. Admission is $8 for adults, $6 for seniors and $4 for children ages 6 to 17. Weekday school tours can be arranged for children of preschool age and older.

Note: Throughout the year on Mondays and Tuesdays, a 2½ hour activity-oriented children's workshop is held for groups in grades 3 through 5. Children explore what it is like to live in the Hill House during the late 19th and early 20th centuries. The planned activities include a scavenger hunt, period sing-a-long and etiquette lessons. Reservations are required. The cost is $200 minimum for a minimum group size of 25. The additional per person fee is $8 fee.

*JAPAN AMERICA SOCIETY OF MINNESOTA (JASM)

Riverplace, Suite EH-131
43 Main St. S.E.
Minneapolis, 55414

612-627-9357
www.mn-japan.org

The society's purpose is to promote an appreciation of cultural, educational, business, public affairs and other interests which bring the peoples of Japan and our community closer together through mutual understanding, respect and cooperation. Membership is open to individuals, organizations and corporations.

Member events are held throughout the year. Tsushin, a monthly newsletter has a calendar listing their many activities and events. It is available on their website. Or contact the society weekdays between 9 AM and 5 PM for membership information and to receive a copy of the Tsushin.

Ask about JASM's Japan in a Suitcase Program that can be scheduled for community and school visits. The suitcase is really a trunk containing Japanese artifacts, books, maps and activities. Availability is dependent on present staffing. A program fee of $50 is requested.

JERRY'S FOOD STORES
Eden Prairie: 9625 Anderson Lake Pkwy., 55344 (952-941-9680)
Edina: 5125 Vernon Ave., 55436 (952-929-2685)

www.jerrysfoods.com

Weekday mornings are the best time to tour one of Jerry's stores. However, arrangements can be made for visits at other times for organized groups such as Scouts, Brownies and Cubs. The deli, meat department, produce, dairy and bakery areas may be seen and explained during the tour that lasts between 30 minutes to an hour. At the bakery, it might be possible to see the cake decorator add the finishing touches to a party cake. At the delivery area, it is impressive to see the paper crusher flatten cardboard boxes into large, compact blocks of paper for recycling. The sausage making operations at the Edina store is explained. Each store offers a different tour as not all stores have the same operations. Groups of 15 are ideal for tours that are best suited for children of grade 2 and up. As reservations in advance are required, contact the nearest store in your area to make arrangements for a tour.

*JONATHAN PADELFORD PACKET BOAT CO., INC.
Harriet Island
St. Paul, 55107

651-227-1100 (infoline)
1-800-543-3908
www.riverrides.com

The Jonathan Padelford sails on the Mississippi from downtown St. Paul's Harriet Island to within sight of Fort Snelling. The Anson Northrup, a sidewheeler, also sails from Harriet Island. Two narrated public cruises are offered daily. One ship sails at noon and another at 2 PM from Memorial Day weekend through Labor Day. During the month of May, school trips can be arranged by reservation. During the month of September, the paddlewheelers sail on Wednesday through Sunday at 2 PM. In October, the days are Friday through Sunday at 2 PM. The trips are from about 90 minutes to 2 hours.

Snacks are available for purchase on the boats. Bring jackets or sweaters as it gets cold on the river even in the summer. Adult tickets are $16, senior tickets are $12 and children ages 3 to 12 are $8. On Mondays, "Monday Madness" day, all tickets are $8.

KITE FLYING
Minnesota Kite Society (MKS)
PO Box 580016
Minneapolis, 55458

www.mnkites.org

Dedicated to the promotion of kite flying throughout the state, many fun and colorful kite flying events are planned throughout the year to do so. The Frosty Fingers Kite Fly is held on Lake Phalen the last weekend of January during St. Paul's Winter Carnival celebration. Other events held traditionally include the Annual Lake Harriet Winter Kite Festival in mid-January and the Flying Colors Kite Festival in August. Their very detailed website lists the flights scheduled throughout the year on the Current Event Calendar.

Annual memberships are available for $20 which includes a newsletter. However, there is no charge for enjoying the outdoor kite flying events

Come Fly With Us!

Note: Special school activities such as a member bringing and talking about different kinds of kites can be arranged. There is no charge for the visits but donations are appreciated to fund these activities.

*LADY ELEGANT'S TEA ROOM
Historic Milton Square
2230 Carter Ave.
St. Paul, 55108

651-645-6676
www.ladyelegantstea.com

Children of 5 and older can partake of a three-course tea party along with instruction in proper tea etiquette at Lady Elegant's Tea Room. Located in an English Tudor building in St. Anthony Park's Milton Square, the setting is perfect for a child's tea party and Mom, Dad, Grandparent or other accompanying adult liking tea, too.

Reservations are required for all the themed parties. Prices range per child from $36 for the Birthday Party to $15 for Tea Time. Each party includes an etiquette lesson. Visit the website, call to request or better yet, stop by for their Let's Have a Tea Party! brochure. The shop is open Wednesday from 11 AM to 2 PM, Thursday and Friday 11 AM to 4 PM and Saturday between 11 AM and 5 PM.

During regular store hours, a child's menu is available along with the adult offerings for those who want to drop by for perhaps a hot cocoa with whipped cream & sprinkles or pot of tea with tasty scones.

Note: The annual American Girl Tea Party is offered the fourth Saturday in September at 11 AM or 2:30 PM. The cost is $20 per person with reservations requested. At this event, children are invited to dressup and bring their favorite doll for tea, an etiquette lesson and a story.

*THE LANDING - MINNESOTA RIVER HISTORIC PARK
Three Rivers Park District
2187 Cty. Hwy. 101 E.
Shakopee, 55379

763-694-7784
www.threeriversparks.org/parks/the-landing

Minnesota life from 1840 to 1890 comes alive upon entering the Landing, known formerly as Historic Murphy's Landing. A walk through the museum begins with a visit to the French fur traders whose life is depicted in the 1840 Faribault cabin. Next, visitors see the Berger's 1850 timbered farm followed by the Ryan's 1860-1880 farm for comparison, then the 1887 one room brick schoolhouse with wood stove and wooden desks and finally a town square typical of those found in a Minnesota River Valley community of German, Czech, Irish or Scandinavian descent. The square has a railroad depot, a general store, a blacksmith shop, a newspaper printing office and a church in addition to residences typical of the 1890s. Since 1969, restoration activities have been underway and continue still with more than 40 historic buildings on the 88-acre site. Interpreters in costumes reflecting the era meet visitors at the restored buildings and explain the types of activities that would go on there. Food preparation, candle dipping, butter churning, soap making, spinning and weaving demonstrations are some of the daily activities shown. On a limited scheduled, a horse-drawn trolley ride acts as a shuttle and is a way for visitors to experience a typical 19th century means of transportation.

Children can play house 1880's style in the Martinson House, one of the newer additions to the museum, through cooking, washing and dress-up with authentic wash tub, pots and pans and try-on clothes of the time.

From Memorial Day through Labor Day, the Landing is open weekends for all their living history event activities from 10 AM to 5 PM Saturday and noon to 5 PM Sunday. There is an event fee of $5 for adults and $3 for seniors and children ages 2 to 17 for participation in the activities. However, in June when guided walking tours are scheduled on the weekends the admission fees are $6 and $5. Parking is free.

The Landing is open and free for self-guided touring on weekends and from 10 AM to 4 PM on weekdays. Visitors, with a self-guided tour brochure available at the Visitor Center, can walk the grounds looking into the building interiors through the windows and glass doors.

Note: Special events are planned year-round including the Living History weekends and in December, the Folkways of the Holidays celebration. It is best to visit their website for the latest news.

LANDMARK CENTER
Across from Rice Park
75 W. 5th St., Suite 404
St. Paul, 55102

651-292-3225 (infoline)
www.landmarkcenter.org

The Landmark Center won an American Institute of Architects award for the beautiful restoration of this 1902 building that originally housed the Federal courts and post office. In 1978 it reopened to become a cultural center for all ages. Walk-in tours are regularly held on Sundays at noon and Thursdays at 11 AM and require no reservations. Meet at the Information Desk. If a special event is being held on Sunday, call 651-292-3225 to confirm noon tour. At other times, ask at the Information Desk if a self-guided tour brochure is available. It is free. And when copies are available, they are written in many non-English languages as well as English.

Throughout the year, there are many Sundays at Landmark programs. Concerts and other family events are held in the center cortile. Columns, a Landmark Center calendar of events, lists the many daily activities and special happenings. Call to receive the mailing. Landmark Center hours vary but it is open every day. For more information about events, please call or visit the website.

Note: Education, school and other special groups with 10 or more children in 4th grade and up can tour by arrangement through calling 651-292-3230. These reservations should be made at least two weeks in advance of desired date. The scheduled tours are 45 minutes. And the fee is $4 per person.

LEGO IMAGINATION CENTER
Mall of America (MOA) South Entrance Level One
Interstate 494 & Hwy. 77
Bloomington, 55425

952-858-8949
www.lego.com

The store's center has several stations for creative play with LEGO and DUPLO blocks. There is the Master Builder area for Star Wars game playing and building. At the Build Your Own Mini-Figures, one has the option to purchase the little figures at 3 for $9.99. Inside the bright red low-walled area with comfortable red benches for adult seating are bright red circular tables each with a pile of blocks for imaginative structure creating on individual green mats.

Gone is the gigantic Clock Tower built of LEGOs. In its place and hovering above are a saber toothed tiger, helicopter and other gigantic LEGO built characters. Look for Toy Story's LEGO Woody. He is popular for posing one's children for a photo.

The center is open Monday through Saturday from 10 AM to 9:30 PM and Sundays from 11 AM to 7 PM.

*LINDER'S GARDEN CENTER
270 W. Larpenteur Ave.
St. Paul, 55113

651-488-1927
www.linders.com

The Sunflower Group meets at 9 AM, the Apple Tree Group at 10:15 AM and the Rose Group at 11:30 AM the 3rd Saturday of each month. These are the names of the Little Sprouts Clubs children ages 4 to 13 can join to learn about gardening through hands-on and educational activities. Each month's meeting has a different theme. The day of our visit Australia and its plant life was explored with maps, photos and some native unusual flowering plants passed among us. The plants with names of kangaroo paw and toothbrush (it has tongue-like flowers) were just two of the many examined. The program was a real "show & tell, touch & smell" fun time. The craft activity for the group was making with clay a boomerang or beads. A small Vegemite sandwich snack was provided to sample, too. Each child went home with a potted pansy plant with care instructions for keeping it alive.

The annual club membership fee is $15 per child and includes a Little Sprouts Club t-shirt, membership badge and birthday gift certificate. And as this is a parent/child program, the adult parent or guardian must remain with the child during the club meeting. Registration is required. The registration form is online on the Little Sprouts page of Linder's website or stop in the store for one. With store hours varying with the season, call or visit the website for when open.

LUNDS AND BYERLEY'S FOOD STORE

Children seem as fascinated by their tour of a Lunds or Byerly's grocery stores as adults who grocery shop here. Groups have come from as far as Duluth to see the fresh fish, taste the pepper cheese and guess what vegetable (maybe a white asparagus?) or fruit (Buddha's citron?) they are being shown. When available, watching the cakes being decorated and/or seeing the unique seafood case with perhaps a whole octopus on display are favorites of tour groups of all ages.

Each store's FoodE (food expert) likes to plan a tour around a certain topic if possible. And she may include other store information such as how merchandise comes into the store and ends up on the shelves and what happens to a shoplifter. Also included may be information on career opportunities in the grocery industry.

Tour days differ among stores. And most prefer the tour be scheduled between 9 AM and 2 PM. Children age 5 and up in groups of up to 20 in size can be accommodated. Reservations made several weeks in advance are a must. A treat is often provided such as a piece of fruit or cookie.

Other special event activities for families with children occur throughout the year. The Drop by the Store on Kids' Days have included in the past clowns, balloons, face painting and I.D. opportunities. Checking the website for scheduled upcoming event details is a great idea.

Bloomington Lunds: 5159 W. 98th St., 55437 (952-896-0092)

Burnsville Byerly's: 401 E. County Rd. 42, 55306 (952-892-5600)

Chanhassen Byerly's: 800 W. 78 St., 55317 (952-474-1298)

Eagan Byerly's: 1299 Promenade Place, 55121 (651-686-9669)

Edina Byerly's: 7171 France Ave. S., 55435 (952-831-3601)

Edina Lunds: 3945 W. 50th St., 55424 (952-926-6833)

Golden Valley Byerly's: 5725 Duluth St., 55422 (763-544-8846)

Maple Grove Byerly's: 12880 Elm Creek Blvd., 55369 (763-416-1611)

Minnetonka Lunds: 11400 Hwy. 7, 55305 (952-935-0198)

Minneapolis Northeast Lunds: 25 University Ave. SE, 55414 (612-548-3820)

Minneapolis Uptown Lunds: 1450 W. Lake St., 55408 (612-825-2440)

Plymouth Lunds: 3455 Vicksburg Lane N., 55447 (763-268-1624)

Richfield Lunds: 6228 Penn Ave. S., 55423 (612-861-1881)

Ridgedale Byerly's: 13081 Ridgedale Dr., 55305 (952-541-1414)

Roseville Byerly's: 1601 W. County Rd. C, 55113 (651-633-6949)

St. Louis Park Byerly's: 3777 Park Center Blvd., 55416 (952-929-2100)

St. Paul Byerly's: 1959 Suburban Ave., 55119 (651-735-6340)

St. Paul Highland Lunds: 2128 Ford Pkwy., St. Paul, 55116 (651-698-5845)

Wayzata Lunds: 1151 Wayzata Blvd. E., 55391 (951-476-2222)

*McDONALD'S RESTAURANTS BIRTHDAY PARTIES & PLAY PLACES

www.mcdonalds.com

Birthday parties are fun to have at McDonald's. A meal, cake and party favors are provided with some restaurants also offering games and a birthday gift. Party costs vary depending on the number of children attending. A few days to 2 weeks notice is needed to schedule a party. Contact the McDonald's restaurant nearest you to inquire if they offer birthday parties or can help you locate one that does.

McDonald's Play Places have playground equipment for children to climb on and romp over while you watch and relax with that last cup of coffee or shake. Use your zipcode on their website to locate the nearest McDonald's and those with a Play Place.

*MACPHAIL CENTER FOR MUSIC
501 S. 2nd St.
Minneapolis, 55401

612-321-0100 (infoline)
www.macphail.org

Sing Play Learn! Help children discover the joys of music through MacPhail Center's Early Childhood Music programs. At MacPhail a child's artistic education can begin as young as 6 weeks. Musical Trolley, just one of the many classes offered for children of all ages, is for children ages 4 through kindergarten. It is about the many instruments of the orchestra. Children can learn about music through movement, listening to and playing instruments. New is the opportunity to schedule (612-767-5505) a free sample class and/or visit a class.

Tuition assistance is available for classes that begin at $235 and up. For information on registration, classes and the other MacPhail locations in White Bear Lake and Apple Valley, call or visit the website.

MAPLEWOOD NATURE CENTER & NEIGHBORHOOD PRESERVES
2659 E. 7th St.
Maplewood, 55119

651-249-2170
www.ci.maplewood.mn.us

This center has an interpretive building that houses reptiles and amphibians in glass cases. There is a children's Touch & See Room with interactive objects such as antlers, horns and furs to feel and examine and books and magazines to read. Animal programs are held for children of preschool age and older. An annual checklist for recording dates of first sightings of birds and animals at the center is kept each year. Classes and programs are free or with small fees from $2 to $5. Pondering the Pond is one of the most popular classes. Registration and class information is available by calling or visiting the center or on the website at Nature Center Events Calendar and Family & Adult Nature Programs.

There is lots going on at this center. There are trails for hiking year round. Or try snowshoeing during the winter. Bring your own or rent at the center for $5 per pair. Sizes are available for ages 3 and up. The paths are fun and easy to follow through the woods and around the pond. Pickup a trail map at the entrance kiosk or in the visitor center and follow the trail rules to spend several enjoyable hours on the grounds. A long boardwalk spans one section of the pond allowing for a good view of pond life below it in warmer months. The trails are open from dawn to dusk. The Visitor Center Building is open from Tuesday through Saturday 8:30 AM to 4:30 PM year around.

Note: Birthday parties can be scheduled at the center for $45 for up to 12 children. Nature hikes, games, activities and favors are provided for entertainment. Reservations are needed. Picnic tables are located on the grounds. A room is available to rent for indoor parties. Party treats are brought by parents.

*MICHAELS KIDS CLUB
Michaels The Arts and Crafts Store

www.michaels.com
www.TheKnackKids.com

The Knack Family Events are Michaels hand-on arts and crafts programs for parents accompanying children of age 3 and older. One new project activity is offered at least monthly in each store's classroom with day and time varying…maybe Tuesday from 10 AM to noon one month; Sunday afternoon from 1 PM to 3 PM another. Often the project has a holiday or seasonal theme like a Valentine's Day puppet or card in February. Some events have a small fee to cover the cost of materials; others are free. The arrangements for attendance are just drop-in…no reservations. For details on current Knack Events, visit their websites or stop by your nearest Michaels for a monthly flyer.

Note: Craft parties can be arranged for birthdays, school groups, scouts and others. Contact your nearest store for a brochure and details. Their Play & Create! Craft Parties for Creative Kids brochure has a selection of projects that begin at $6 per child.

*MILL CITY MUSEUM
Minnesota Historical Society (MHS)
704 2nd St. S.
Minneapolis, 55401

612-341-7555 (infoline)
www.millcitymuseum.org

Did you know that from 1880 to 1930 Minneapolis was known as the Flour Capital of the World. And the Washburn A Mill was the most technically advanced and largest in the world until replace by the Pillsbury Mill on the other side of the river.

Restored and operated by the MHS, the mill opened as a museum in 2003. Look for the Gold Medal Flour outdoor sign when going for a visit. The museum is located next door to it.

Today, there are many hands-on activities that children of ages 6 and older will find of interest and fun. There is the Water Lab, the Baking Lab and the Flour Tower Show, a must experience. The show is a 12-minute elevator ride that travels 8 floors stopping at several for viewing reconstructed rooms depicting life in the mill when in operation. Recorded messages tell the Washburn mill's story throughout the ride. And the attraction, Minneapolis in 19 Minutes Flat, is a combination live action and animated film history of the city for viewing for ages of kindergarten and older.

The Charles H. Bell Ruin Courtyard is of interest as it shows remains of the mill's limestone walls left open to the sky.

Finally be sure to climb the stairs or ride an elevator to the 9th floor indoor/outdoor observation deck. The view looking east over the Mississippi River is spectacular.

Museum admission is adults $10, seniors $8, children 6 to 17 $5 and age 5 and under free. The museum hours are Tuesday through Saturday 10 AM to 5 PM except Thursday when open until 9 PM. Sunday hours are noon to 5 PM.

Note: Education groups and other groups of 10 or more can select from planned program activities for visits to the museum. The programs are for preschool age and up. Each program includes the very popular self-guided Scavenger Hunt activity. Pricing of programs depend on the program package selected. The fees per person begin at $5 for youth groups and $6 for students attending a People, Power or Flour themed field trip. Registration is required at least 2 weeks in advance and can be made by calling the museum scheduler (612-341-7556) or on online on the website. Additional information including descriptions of the different programs and pricing for each is on the website and/or by contacting the museum scheduler.

MINNEAPOLIS INSTITUTE OF ARTS (MIA)
2400 3rd Ave. S.
Minneapolis, 55404

612-870-3131 (infoline)
1-888-642-2787
www.artsmia.org

One of the most enjoyable places for children to go for exploring the different art forms is the MIA. Presently one of the offerings, Art Carts, is a themed collection on a cart of musical instruments to play, clothing to try on and specially selected art items to handle. The Art Carts may have a tie-in to the institute's current special exhibit…like the previous ones on China and Medieval Arts. On the website select Education & Resources for the themes of the current Art Carts and other details including scheduled times and gallery locations. Another program, Art Adventures, is for students in kindergarten to 6th grades. In this program, parent volunteers with training provided by the institute, visit classrooms.

New is the Artful Stories: a Preschool Tour event for ages 3 to 5. Also school group tours and custom tours for 10 or more children of kindergarten age and up and are offered. Make reservation at least 4 weeks prior to a desired tour date. A list of suggested tour topics is on MIA's website as well as a printable mailable tour request form. Tour information is also available by calling the tour office at 612-870-3140.

Admission to the institute is free. However, some special exhibits do charge an admission for entry. The institute is open Tuesday through Saturday from 10 AM to 5 PM except on Thursday evenings when it is open until 9 PM. Sundays the institute is open from noon to 5 PM. It is closed on Mondays. For parents with children of infant age to 7 in need of a break, a Family Center is located on the first floor.

Note: One Sunday each month between 11 AM and 4:30 PM, MIA has a free Family Day art happening event. The dates and themes for these along with the planned activities are located by selecting Current Events option on MIA's website.

MINNEAPOLIS PARK & RECREATION BOARD (MP&RB)
2117 W. River Rd.
Minneapolis, 55411

612-230-6400
http://www.minneapolisparks.org

Minneapolis has 50 excellent community and neighborhood centers. In 1989 MP&RB was named the winner of the National Gold Medal Award at the National Recreation & Park Association Congress, an award honoring excellence in park and recreational management. And in 2010, the Commission for Accreditation of Parks & Recreation Agencies (CAPRA) was received recognizing excellence in operations and services.

Programs, classes and recreational activities are planned for preschoolers throughout the year at each center. For elementary age children, arts & crafts classes, dance, active games and sports programs are scheduled for after school, Saturdays and on week days during the summer months at most centers. Neighborhood Naturalist Programs are offered at some of the centers. The programs have environmental educational themes and activities such as learning about squiggly and squirmy bugs, snakes and worms or using recycled materials to make nature art. Some of the classes have small fees for materials or instruction costs. Visit the website or ask at your nearest center for current and upcoming activities and special events.

The park board encourages residents with children to use the beaches, boat docks, fishing docks, picnic areas and hiking and biking trails. During the summer, swimming lessons are offered at some of the beaches, at the 2 new water parks and Webber Pool. During the winter months, there are ski lessons, snowboarding and snow tubing at Theodore Wirth as well as skating and hockey rinks at many centers. During the season, for weather condition updates call 612-313-7708 (infoline).

MINNEAPOLIS SCULPTURE GARDEN
1750 Hennepin Ave.
Vineland Place across from Walker Art Center at Lyndale &
Hennepin Aves.
Minneapolis, 55403

612-375-7609 (tour office infoline)
www.walkerart.org

The Minneapolis Sculpture Garden is located on 11 acres of land. On display are more than 40 sculptures divided among four 100-foot square plazas with walking paths defining the spaces. Favorites of families include the huge Spoonbridge and Cherry sculpture located in the gardens and the 65-foot tall Standing Glass Fish in the Cowles Conservatory. In the Judy and Kenneth Dayton Sculpture Plaza, children, with a boost up, can gently swing on the Arikidea sculpture's rope platform and climb through the Ordovician Pore. A free and very informative garden guide brochure is available in the conservatory. Pick one up. There are lots to see and talk about when visiting this unique and popular attraction.

The garden is open from 6 AM to midnight every day of the year. The conservatory hours are Tuesday through Sunday from 11 AM until 5 PM with the exception of Thursday when open until 9 PM.

Walk-in tours are offered on weekends at 1 PM May through September. Meet the tour guide in the Walker Art Center lobby. No reservations are needed. Call for information on scheduling a group tour.

Note: A backpack, called a WAC Pack, has games and activities for families to use in exploring the gardens. It can be checked out with paid admission at the Walker Art lobby desk.

MINNEHAHA DEPOT
Minnesota Transportation Museum (MTM)
In Minnehaha Park near Highway 55 & Minnehaha Parkway
Minneapolis, 55417

651-228-0263 (infoline)
www.mtmuseum.org
www.mnhs.org/places/sites/md/index.html

This is one of the last Victorian-style railway stations left in Minnesota. It was built in the mid-1870s and is known as The Princess because of its delicate gingerbread architecture. Today the depot is open Sunday afternoons and holidays from 2 PM to 6 PM from Memorial Day through Labor Day and during the school year by reservation. Operated by MTM, additional information can be had by calling or visiting the websites.

MINNEHAHA FALLS & PARK
Minnehaha Pkwy. along the Mississippi River
Minneapolis, 55417

The falls was immortalized by Longfellow in his poem, *The Song of Hiawatha*, and is an enjoyable place to visit throughout the year. In the winter, the falls are frozen into fascinating patterns. In the summer, a flight of steps can be followed to a landing just below the falls. A statue of Hiawatha is located above the falls.

MINNESOTA AIR GUARD MUSEUM
ANG Base at Minneapolis & St. Paul International Airport
670 Gen. Miller Drive at Hwys. 62 & 55
PO Box 11598
St. Paul, 55111

612-713-2523
www.mnangmuseum.org

The museum is located on the Minnesota Air National Guard base in the northeast corner of the airport near Ft. Snelling. Vintage aircraft, pictures, memorabilia and artifacts tell the story of the Minnesota's 109th Aero Squadron from its beginning in 1921 to the present. And the oldest planes at the museum date back to the late 1930s. There are now 20 aircraft on display in the airpark including an F-16 fighting jet, the Fighting Falcon, originally flown out of the Duluth Air Base. One learns from the museum staff that the F-16 is also currently being flown throughout and over 30 countries including Afghanistan and Iraq. Visit the website for current calendar of events.

The museum is open for public tours mid-April through mid-September most Saturdays from 11 AM to 4 PM. There is no fee for public tours but donations are welcome. Private booked tours at other times throughout the year can be arranged for groups of 6 or more for $7 adults and $5 for children 6 and over. Call during office hours of 9 AM to 2 PM Tuesday through Friday and Saturday 11 AM to 4 PM to schedule a private tour. All visitors must arrive by car. All persons 18 and older must have a picture ID.

Note: Birthday parties at a suggested price of $100 can be booked. The program planned for a party includes a private tour and goody bags. The birthday child receives a disposable camera for taking memorable pictures. The goodies to be eaten are brought from home.

*MINNESOTA CENTER FOR BOOK ARTS (MCBA)
1011 Washington Ave. So.
Minneapolis, 55415

612-215-2520 (infoline)
www.mnbookarts.org

The center offers seasonal classes and events in papermaking, bookmaking and printing. They are designed for children ages 2 and up. A recent class created a holiday card with the center's paper pulp and molds along with beads, ribbons, photographs, etc. brought from home. Family classes are on Saturdays with special events on other days also. Some events are free; others have fees ranging from $24 to $36 with discounts for members and some are limited in size. Call for a seasonal brochure or visit the website for the current offerings.

Youth workshops and field trips are available at MCBA, too. They are of 1 to 3 hours long and include an introduction to the world of book arts and a hands-on activity. This could include making a book, making paper or printing a page. An extensive class listing by grade appropriate ages is on the website. A fee from $5.25 and up per person is charged with a group minimum cost that depends on the selected project. Groups up to 100 can be accommodated. Reservations are required. Contact the Youth Programs coordinator at 612-215-2529 for arrangements.

*MINNESOTA DEPARTMENT OF NATURAL RESOURCES (DNR)
DNR License & Information Center
500 Lafayette Rd.
St. Paul, 55155

651-296-6157
1-888-646-6367
www.dnr.state.mn.us

An year-round vehicle park permit for unlimited visits to all 72 Minnesota state parks and recreation areas can be purchased for $25 or a one-day permit for $5. The vehicle permit sticker can be purchased at all state parks, at the DNR center and at other Twin City locations listed on the web.

The DNR website is one of the best for ease of use. Choices include find a Park by a list A-Z, Kids Programs, Events and Destinations among others. It even provides access to the current weather conditions in St. Paul with option to change city location at **www.dnr.state.mn.us/current_conditions/index.html**

*MINNESOTA HISTORY CENTER (MHC)
Minnesota Historical Society (MHS)
345 Kellogg Blvd. W.
St. Paul, 55102

651-259-3000 (infoline)
1-800-657-3773 (infoline)
www.mnhs.org/historycenter

Did you know that Minnesota gets its name from the Dakota Indian word "minisota" which means sky-tinted waters? Did you know that Minnesota waters flow in three directions: north to Canada's Hudson Bay, east to the Atlantic Ocean and south to the Gulf of Mexico and that no water flows into the state?

With the mission of the Society to collect, preserve, interpret and exhibit Minnesota history, these and other interesting history facts can be discovered when visiting the History Center.

Special family day events are occasionally held throughout the year usually on a weekend afternoon. At each of these History HiJinx programs a hands-on, take-home activity is planned for children and families. The activity is history related to the theme of the event so they learn about Minnesota history. So far children have learned a game for collecting their family's stories plus make a treasure chest to keep them in and have built miniature shimmering ice palaces among many other fun projects. The activity has no added fee. The project's materials are provided. No reservation is needed.

The MHC **www.mnhs.org/fieldtrips** offers a variety of school field trips programs for prekindergarten age children and older. Costs begin at $5 per person. Registration is possible on the website or by calling the tour scheduling office (651-259-3400).

The center is open Tuesday through Saturday from 10 AM to 5 PM except on Tuesday evening when it is open until 8 PM. Sunday the center is open from noon until 5 PM. Admission is $10 for adults, $8 for seniors and college students and $5 for children 6 to 17. From 5 PM to 8 PM Tuesdays admission is free. Library admission is free. Parking is $5 and $3 for members.

MINNESOTA STATE CAPITOL BUILDING TOUR
Minnesota Historical Society (MHS)
75 Rev. Dr. Martin Luther King Jr. Blvd.
At Aurora & Park Ave.
St. Paul, 55155

651-296-2881 (infoline)
www.mnhs.org/places/sites/msc

The capitol is located just a few blocks north of downtown St. Paul in the Capitol Complex area. Architect Cass Gilbert designed our marble dome to be similar to that of the capitol's dome in Washington, D.C. Opened in 1905, the State Capitol houses the chambers for the 2 branches of State Legislature, the Governor's office and the Supreme Court. The website **www.leg.state.mn.us/leg/youth** has Links for Youth with a selection of options. One of these, Symbols, has a State Symbols option. Click on it to find a game and Just for Fun printable pages for coloring.

On a tour, one hears about the capitol's history, art and architecture, visits the government chambers and weather allowing, can walk to the capitol's roof to see the golden horses.

Regularly scheduled free guided tours lasting about 45 minutes leave hourly from 10 AM to 2 PM on Monday through Saturday and at 1, 2, 3 PM on Sundays. Groups of 10 or more require reservations of 2 weeks in advance that can be made by calling 651-296-2881 or by email online. Another tour option, the printable self-guided tour brochure, is on the web for those who want to tour at their leisure or other times.

Educational group tours of 15 or more for preschool children and older require reservations at least 2 weeks in advance by calling 651-296-2881.

A minimum fee of $75 is charged for the themed 90 minute tours. The website has a listing of all the selections and details.

Special events are held at the capitol throughout the year. Mainly planned for adults and older children, these all have admission fees that require prepayment and reservations. The website includes all the details.

The state capitol building hours are Monday through Friday 9 AM to 5 PM, Saturday 10 AM to 3 PM and Sunday 1 PM to 4 PM.

Note: On a family visit, purchase the Art Treasures in the Minnesota State Capitol booklet at the Information Desk for $2. Use it for a scavenger hunt activity. Find items such as the griffin and Colonel Colvill's statue plus 10 others. Record the finding with a gold sticker star. Don't forget to stop back at the Information Desk upon completion to collect the special seal reward for finding all of them.

MINNESOTA VALLEY NATIONAL WILDLIFE REFUGE
3815 American Blvd. E.
Bloomington, 55425

952-854-5900
www.fws.gov/midwest/minnesotavalley

Described as one of the best-kept secrets in the Twin Cities, this wildlife center needs to be discovered. It is open 9 AM to 5 PM Tuesday through Sunday, April through October and the first full weekend of each month from 9 AM to 4 PM November through March; closed on Mondays and holidays. The interpretive and education center was built for the U.S. Fish and Wildlife Service in 1990. It has a hiking trail that leads to a marsh in the valley. A multi-level exhibition hall has many hands-on exhibits for children to try. Through visiting the exhibits, one can learn how the river valley was formed and all about the refuge's grasslands and marshlands and river channel.

The center offers free educational programs for children of kindergarten age and older. Visit the website or call for information on these.

*MINNETONKA CENTER FOR THE ARTS (MCA)
2240 North Shore Dr.
Wayzata, 55391

952-473-7361 (infoline)
www.minnetonkaarts.org

During the school year, Saturdays are special days for children at the center with additional classes now also offered weekdays and Tuesday evenings as well. Workshops and classes in drawing, paints, clay, collage and sculpting are for children ages 5 and up. Fees for children's classes begin at $84 and workshop fees begin at $29. With membership, there is a discount. There are additional materials fee.

A catalog with all the free activities and events as well as workshops and class offerings is available. Call to inquire about receiving one. The website also contains current information on all the classes, shows and exhibits at the center. Through calling or visiting the website, one will also receive information about Art Birthday parties arrangements at MCA and classes for preschool age children and up now offered at MCA's new Ridgedale location.

The center hours are Monday, Friday and Saturday 9 AM to 5 PM and Tuesday through Thursday from 9 AM to 9:30 PM. Summer Saturday hours are 9 AM to 1 PM.

Note: MCA Summer Arts Camp is designed to allow children ages 5 to 15 years old to explore various media including drawing, jewelry, clay and fabric art. There is much flexibility in session lengths to allow for all the other activities going on during the summer. Half-day sessions start at $33 for non-members and $30 for members. Contact the center for all the details.

MUSEUM ADVENTURE PASS
Presented by Macy's
www.melsa.org/museumadventurepass

Check online or at your local MELSA library for the guidelines on how to check out a Museum Adventure Pass. The pass can be exchanged for 2 free admissions to over 15 local Twin Cities museums.

*NICKELODEON UNIVERSE
5500 Center Court
Mall of America (MOA)
Interstate 494 & Hwy. 77
Bloomington, 55425

952-883-8600 (infoline)
www.nickelodeonuniverse.com
www.moa.com

Nickelodeon Universe is a unique indoor amusement and entertainment park located in the Center Court of MOA. Designed with children and families in mind, it is a nice alternative for those days when the outdoors is not. There are lots of trees, benches and walking spaces here, too. The park is mainly for rides and eats. There are over 25 rides and attractions. Single points cost $1 each for a pay-as-you-play point pass on individual rides. Admission ride packages are available including a $29.95 wristband allowing for unlimited rides for a day. Hours open are 10 AM to 7:30 PM or later depending on day of the week.

Note: Birthdays can be celebrated here for a group of 10 or more. No reservations are taken but party must check in at Guest Relations on the main floor next to the carousel to purchase the Birthday Party Package. The cost is $19.95 per person and includes a wristband good for 5 hours of rides, a Dippin' Dots ice cream treat and a gift bag. Visit the website for details or call 952-883-8555.

*NORTHERN CLAY CENTER (NCC)
2424 Franklin Ave. E.
Minneapolis, 55406

612-339-8007 (infoline)
www.northernclaycenter.org

Hands-on clay events for ages 6 and older can be arranged with 3 weeks advance notice required. Children will make a clay project and glaze it. The item is fired and ready for pick up to take home a few weeks later. Possible projects include a mask, vase, treasure box and of course, the always can't have enough, mug. This two hour event is $175 for up to 10 people. This could be a good birthday party event, too.

The NCC offers a free guided tour with advance 3 week notice. Also a wheel demonstration is available for $35. During the demo, an artist creates pots on the potter's wheel.

The NCC has Clay for Families classes beginning at $145. Try Throwing Together for ages 9 and up. One-day events begin at $45. Try Mug Shots an event also for adult and child age 6 and up to do together.

The center is open Tuesday through Saturday from 10 AM to 6 PM and Sunday from noon to 4 PM. Closed Mondays. Contact the center to request a clay events brochure and class listing newsletter or visit the website. Parking is convenient in lot adjacent to building.

Note: Clay Camp for children 6 to 16 is a summer camp experience. Tuition ranges from $160 to $290. Dinosaurs Unearthed is one offering and The Gnomes of Verona, another. For details, contact NCC.

*NSC MINNESOTA STARS
National Sports Center
1700 105th Ave. NE
Blaine, 55449

763-792-7355

www.nscminnesota.com

Professional soccer is back. The Twin Cities is fortunate to have the Minnesota Stars, a very successful team that also goes out of its way to encourage and promote local youth soccer. The Stars are a member of the North American Soccer League (NASL) that includes among others teams Tampa Bay, Montreal and Puerto Rico.

The season extends from April through August with home games usually held on Saturday evenings at 7:30 PM. Fans of all ages are invited onto the field after games to meet and greet the players. Visit the website for the current schedule of games, directions to the stadium, team news and information on soccer camps.

Online ticket prices begin at $6 for youth ages 17 and under and $12 for adults. Walkup tickets begin at $8 and $14. Parking is free.

Notes: Kids Day, an annual event held at 11 AM on a Wednesday in late June, is special. On this day, ticket prices are $5 for all ages. In addition, there are children's games and prizes. Youth soccer clubs are invited to participate in Club Night programs. One of the features of the program is the opportunity to serve as ball kids. There are also pregame field events for the participating club. Contact the Stars to join the club.

*OMNITHEATER
Located in the Science Museum of Minnesota
120 W. Kellogg Blvd.
St. Paul, 55102

651-221-9444 (infoline)
www.smm.org

The William L. McKnight-3M Omnitheater is one of the most popular attractions in the Twin Cities. The world's largest film projector, the Omnimax, projects 70 mm film onto a rotating dome giving the viewer the feeling of being in the middle of the projected action. This could be hang gliding over the surf of the Big Sur or riding in a hot air balloon over a New England church steeple or careening down a snowy trail in northern Minnesota on a snowmobile. The showtimes are on the hour beginning at 10 AM or 11 AM until 9 PM on weekends and 1 PM and 2 PM weekdays.

The show lasts about one hour.

As the Omni is so popular, especially on Sunday afternoons, arrive early to purchase tickets. They are $8 for adults and $7 for seniors and children 4 to 12. Tickets can also be purchased online on the website. Reservations can be made for an additional $3 per ticket by calling 651-221-9444 at least two hours in advance. For current show information and times, visit the website or call the infoline.

Note: School groups of elementary and secondary ages can arrange weekday morning ShowTimes and receive special rates by contacting the Omni in advance of the planned visit. These arrangements are subject to theater availability.

*ORCHESTRA HALL
The Minnesota Orchestra
1111 Nicollet Mall
Minneapolis, 55403

1-800-292-4141 (infoline)
612-371-5656
www.minnesotaorchestra.org

The Minnesota Orchestra presents each year an Adventures in Music for Families series of concerts called Target Free Family Concerts. Recommended for children ages 11 and under, the performances are at 2 PM and 4 PM on four Sunday afternoons, usually between September and May. This is an wonderful way for families to explore music together. Free tickets are distributed through a random drawing. Check **www.minnesotaorchestra.org/target** or call 612-31-5656 for more information on the registration period and other details on these concerts.

Young People's Concerts is another musical experience. These concerts are designed for school children of elementary age and older, scheduled on weekdays at 10 AM and 11:35 AM and usually about one hour long. Each school year, a series of unique programs are planned. Examples of programs have included Swinging Nutcracker, Beethoven's Fifth and At the Movies with the Minnesota Orchestra. Schools and educational groups can see all the details at **www.minnesotaorchestra.org/yp** or through calling group ticket sales at 612-371-5671 weekdays from 9 AM to 5 PM. Group prices are $6 per ticket. Reservations begin in April for the following school year.

Another extremely popular program is the WAMSO Kinder Konzerts. These are designed for children 4 and 5 years old who come with a preschool or nursery school or adult. The programs are short and fun. They are held on 12 different weekday mornings throughout the school year at 9 AM and 11 AM. The cost is $5 per attendee. One adult is free when accompanied by 5 children. To request a brochure describing the details, contact the WAMSO office (612-371-5654) Monday through Thursday from 9 AM to 4 PM or visit their website **www.wamso.org**

*ORDWAY CENTER FOR THE PERFORMING ARTS
Education and Community Engagement at Ordway
345 Washington St.
St. Paul, 55102

651-282-3115 (infoline)
www.ordway.org/education

The Ordway's education staff plans a series of 15 performing arts programs for young people each school year. At 10:30 AM and 12:30 PM, the series includes multi-cultural dance and music performances. Students from kindergarten through grade 12 may attend. Tickets range from $3 to $6 per person per program. Start planning for these programs in late summer as they are very popular and reservations made well in advance are a must.

*PAVEK MUSEUM OF BROADCASTING
3515 Raleigh Ave.
St. Louis Park, 55416

952-926-8198
www.museumofbroadcasting.com

This museum's beginnings date back to 1919 when Joseph R. Pavek built a crystal receiving set and a Model T Ford spark coil transmitter. Today, the museum houses thousands of radio sets, transmitters and broadcasting station equipment as well as a library of books on electricity, magnetism and other subjects related to the development of the radio.

The museum is open to the public year around Wednesday through Saturday from 10 AM to 5 PM. It is closed Sunday through Tuesday. Call to arrange for special tours or large group visits. The website has information on upcoming events, educational opportunities and a location map. Admission is $6 for adults and $5 for students and seniors. It is suggested that children in grades 4 and above will find the museum's displays of most interest.

If you enjoyed the Bakken Museum, you will want to visit this one too.

PINE TREE APPLE ORCHARD
450 Apple Orchard Rd.
White Bear Lake, 55110

651-429-7202 (infoline)
www.pinetreeappleorchard.com

In September and October, a guided tour of the orchards at Pine Tree may be arranged through reservations made in advance. During busy times when guided tours are not possible, groups can go on self-guided tours and see where apple sorting, the cider press operations, etc. are located. Judging from the many thank you letters written by children and posted on a wall in the salesroom, the touring is fun. We enjoy going to the special weekend events held in the fall which have included in past years wagon rides, pick your own pumpkin and a corn maze. Open from mid-June through March, a trip to this orchard to pick your own strawberries beginning in mid-June and to buy apples, cider, pie or apple donuts beginning in August has always been an enjoyable experience for our family.

Located off E. Hwy. 96 in a woodsy setting, getting to this orchard is part of the fun. Watch carefully for their signs! As hours very with the season, you are advised to call or visit the website before going.

*THE PLANETARIUM & OBSERVATORY

Astronomy and space sciences are of interest to all ages. We are fortunate to have several local places we can go to see and to learn more through the programs and events each offers. These locations can be visited for their night star gazing, star shows or sky education events:

*Como Planetarium** in Como Elemenatry School, 780 W. Wheelock Pky., St. Paul, 55117, 651-293-5398 (infoline) **www.planetarium.spps.org** Public visits selected Thursdays and school field trips and scout shows. Admission $5 per person. Here is "where things are always looking up."

Eisenhower Observatory in Eisenhower Community Center, 1001 Hwy. 7, Hopkins, 55305, 952-988-4074 **www.hopkins.k12.mn.us** Search on "observatory." Public visits and school field trips. Donations of $2 adults and $1 students accepted.

*Onan Observatory** in Baylor Regional Park (952-466-5250), 10775 Cty. Rd. 33, Norwood/Young America, 55397 **www.mnastro.org/onan** 952-467-2426 (infoline). Free monthly public star gazing events April through November weather permitting. Park entry requires daily fee or annual pass.

Let the Stars Shine for You!

POLICE STATIONS

Most police stations welcome visits by young children. During a visit, police officers like to emphasize their role in helping people in the community. The officers like to talk to children about the importance of safety when riding a bicycle and walking in the street. In Minneapolis, contact the Commander of one of these 5 precinct stations to arrange a visit: 612-673-5701 for Precinct 1, 612-673-5702 for Precinct 2, 612-673-5703 for Precinct 3, 612-673-5704 for Precinct 4 or 612-673-5705 for Precinct 5. It is best to call between the hours of 8 AM and 4 PM.

In St. Paul, police officer visits can be arranged by requesting in writing the date, time, place for the visit, ages of the children and topics of interest to be covered. The request should be addressed to the Chief of Police, 367 Grove St., St. Paul, 55101. Additional questions can be answered by calling 651-266-5588 weekdays.

Most other communities when contacted will help arrange a visit to their building. Some police departments will arrange school visits also.

Note: 5TH PRECINCT STATION, 3101 Nicollet Ave. S., Minneapolis, 55408 (612-673-5705) has on exhibit in display cases a small collections of weapons and photographs. There is no longer a need to contact the station to make arrangements for a visit. Just drop by to see them.

NOTES

RAMSEY COUNTY HISTORICAL SOCIETY (RCHS)
323 Landmark Center
75 W. 5th St.
St. Paul, 55102

651-222-0701
www.rchs.com

"Exploring history close to home" is the theme of RCHS. One of its main attractions is the Gibbs Museum, the oldest remaining farmhouse in Ramsey County, where special programs and events are held throughout the year for families and children's groups. Discover more information about the museum in the G's, its alphabetical location. To receive a seasonal calendar of all the RCHS events, contact the society weekdays during the office hours of 9 AM to 5 PM or visit their website to locate the Latest RCHS News.

RAMSEY COUNTY LIBRARY
Administrative Offices
4570 Victoria St.
Shoreview, 55126

651-486-2200
www.rclreads.org

Children under 18 years of age can receive a library card with a parent or guardian providing assistance through presenting current picture and current address identification. There are no age restrictions. Books, talking books, magazines, DVDs and CDs can be checked out. Most materials are loaned for 3 weeks. DVDs are loaned for 1 week. Overdue childrens items are 10 cents per day per item except for DVDs that are $1 per day.

Storytimes are held frequently for toddlers and preschool age children at all libraries. Maplewood and Roseville libraries have Baby & Me, a program for babies as young as 6 months. Summer reading programs for children are scheduled at all libraries.

As the hours vary from library to library, contact the nearest one for these. And then visit to pickup a Library Guide brochure and a copy of their seasonal publication, ExpLORE Your Guide to News & Events. The website contains much of this information as well.

MAPLEWOOD: 3025 Southlawn Dr., 55109 (651-704-2033)

MOUNDS VIEW: 2576 Cty. Rd. 10, 55112 (651-717-3272)

NEW BRIGHTON: 400 10th St. NW, 55112 (651-724-6002)

NORTH ST. PAUL: 2290 N 1st St., 55109 (651-747-2700)

ROSEVILLE: 2180 N. Hamline Ave., 55113 (651-628-6803)
SHOREVIEW: 4570 N. Victoria St., 55126 (651-486-2300)
WHITE BEAR LAKE: 4698 Clark Ave., 55110 (651-407-5302

RAMSEY COUNTY PARKS & RECREATION DEPT.
2015 N. Van Dyke St.
Maplewood, 55109

651-748-2500
www.co.ramsey.mn.us/parks

The parks and recreation areas in Ramsey County are used for many children's activities. Swimming, boating, hiking, fishing, picnicking and cross-country skiing are available in most of the parks. Skating instruction is offered at several ice arenas including the Charles M. Schulz-Highland Ice Arena. For more information on the use of the parks and recreation areas and skating instruction, call or write the department or visit the website and subscribe to Announcements and News delivered via email. The office hours are 8 AM to 4:30 PM Monday through Friday.

Note: Battle Creek **Waterworks Family Aquatic Center** is an outdoor water park open from early June through mid-August from late morning to early evening. It is located at 2401 Upper Afton Rd. in Battle Creek Regional Park. Admission is $6.50 for all ages. Visit the website **www.co.ramsey.mn.us/parks/waterpark** or call for current seasonal information.

THE RED BALLOON BOOKSHOP
Children's Books, Etc.
891 Grand Ave.
St. Paul, 55105

651-224-8320
1-888-224-8320
www.redballoonbookshop.com

Storytimes are regularly scheduled on Tuesday mornings at 10:30 AM for babies, Thursday mornings at 10:30 AM for toddlers and Wednesday mornings at 10:30 AM for preschoolers. Held in a corner of the bookshop, these are an excellent opportunity to introduce children to the love for reading. Events on Saturday mornings at 10:30 AM have a different program each time. Other events for children and families are offered throughout the year. All have connections to reading and books. A newsletter of the events is available in the bookshop and on the website. The bookshop is open seven days a week.

ST. PAUL CHAMBER ORCHESTRA (SPCO)
The Historic Hamm Building 3rd Floor
408 St. Peter St.
St. Paul, 55102

651-292-3243
www.thespco.org

During each orchestra season, SPCO offers Ordway Family Concerts for young people ages 3 to 12. Start the Music! is a program for families with young children ages 3 to 6. For this event, SPCO plans a new 30 minute concert to introduce children to a classical music experience through interacting with the music, the musicians and their instruments. Another program, xplorchestra! concerts, is for ages 6 to 12. Members of the orchestra participate with the attendees in exploring a musical travel adventure together. Come early for the hands-on activities prior to each concert.

All concerts are at 9:30 AM and 11:00 AM on Saturday mornings on the third floor of the Hamm Building. Tickets are free through random drawing registration. For registration information, contact SPCO's ticket office (651-291-1144) and/or visit the website **www.thespco.org** click on Upcoming Concerts and select Concerts/Tickets to locate Free Family Music.

ST. PAUL PARKS & RECREATION DEPT.
400 City Hall Annex
25 W. 4th St.
St. Paul, 55102

651-266-6400 (infoline)
www.stpaul.gov/parks

St. Paul has 25 recreation centers and recommends contacting the closest one in your community for a schedule of its planned activities. Como Park offers downhill ski lessons for children ages 4 and older. Como Park also has cross-country skiing lessons and rentals. Registration with fees for instruction are required. Swimming programs are offered during the summer at the outdoor pools and Phalen beach. Fees are charged for swim lessons. All pools have open swim with admission fees of $6.50 adults, $6 seniors and $5 for ages 16 and under with children 48 inches and under $4.50. Discounted swim passes are also available.

Note: **Great River Water Park**, Oxford Community Center, 270 N. Lexington Pkwy. (651-642-0650) can be enjoyed year around. The large kiddie pool features a wooden raft with sprayers and slides. Select Oxford Community Center on the website for information on hours, admission fees and special events.

ST. PAUL PUBLIC LIBRARY
Central Library
90 W. 4th St.
St. Paul, 55102

651-266-7000 (infoline)
www.sppl.org

Children's books and most other library materials can be borrowed for 3 weeks with a library card. Children of any age can have a card. A parent, guardian or teacher can assist the very young child in obtaining his or her card. The Central Library has a wonderful Youth Services Room (651-266-7034). They and many other libraries have children's programs during the school year. All libraries have storytimes and summer reading programs. Pamphlets and brochures identifying the many reading activities including lists of recommended books are available in all the libraries. As the libraries have varying hours, check with the library before a visit. Or better still pick up the Map & Hours brochure available at every library or visit the website. Each has a map of all locations with their hours open.

ARLINGTON HILLS: 1105 Greenbrier St., 55106 (651-793-3930)

CENTRAL: 90 W. 4th St., 55102 (651-266-7000)

DAYTON'S BLUFF: 645 E. 7th St., 55106 (651-793-1699)

HAMLINE MIDWAY: 1558 W. Minnehaha, 55104 (651-642-0293)

HAYDEN HEIGHTS: 1456 White Bear Ave., 55106 (651-793-3934)

HIGHLAND PARK: 1974 Ford Pky., 55116 (651-695-3700)

MERRIAM PARK: 1831 Marshall Ave., 55104 (651-642-0385)

RICE STREET: 1011 Rice St., 55117 (651-558-2223)

RIVERVIEW: 1 E. George St., 55107 (651-292-6626)

RONDO COMMUNITY OUTREACH: 461 N. Dale St., 55104
(651-266-7400)

ST. ANTHONY PARK: 2245 Como Ave., 55108 (651-642-0411)

SUN RAY: 2105 Wilson, 55119 (651-501-6300)

WEST SEVENTH: 265 Oneida St., 55102 (651-298-5516)

Note: At the Central Library, Saturday Live with performers like puppeteers and magicians present a free program for families with children of all ages at 11:15 AM.

St. Paul Public operates a Bookmobile that visits many city locations on a bi-weekly schedule. For information on these locations and scheduled times, contact the Bookmobile office at 651-266-7450 or on website select Locations and Hours and click on Bookmobile.

ST. PAUL REGIONAL WATER SERVICES (SPRWS)
McCarron Treatment Plant
1900 Rice St. N.
Maplewood, 55113

651-266-6350
www.ci.stpaul.mn.us/water

Guided tours for school groups of 6th grade age and up can be arranged. During the tour, students see and are told about the processing of our surface water as it flows through the treating, filtering and pumping steps. It is best to schedule the visit at a time when class is studying water science.

Note: A public tour is offered in the fall or spring during the SPRWS's Open House. Check the website or call for the date of the next one.

*ST. PAUL SAINTS BASEBALL TEAM
Midway Stadium
1771 Energy Park Dr.
St. Paul, 55108

651-644-6659
www.saintsbaseball.com

The St. Paul Saints baseball team plays in an outdoor stadium to fans of all ages. They are in the American Association League with teams from Sioux City IA, Sioux Falls SD, Fargo ND, Fort Worth TX and others. The season begins in early May and ends in early September. Most games are at 7:05 PM except on Sunday when most start at 1:05 PM. Tickets cost from $5 to $12. But tickets in advance to avoid the $1 per ticket fee when purchasing on game day.

The Saints organization provides more than a ballgame to attendees. The game might be followed by all-star wrestling, fireworks and on-field autograph sessions. Between innings, a wedding could take place as it did one of the evenings we attended. Promotional activities include giveaways of baseball cards, bats and logo balls. And don't forget to wave at the trains. If lucky, you might catch one tooting their horn. All of the events are fun and planned with families in mind.

Note: Saints Kids Club is free. Join online and receive the monthly Kid's Club E-Newsletter, voucher for 5 free Sunday home games, an autographed Mudonna baseball card and more.

THE SCHUBERT CLUB MUSEUM
Rice Park
Landmark Center
75 W. 5th St.
St. Paul, 55102

651-292-3267
www.schubert.org/museum

Located on the 2nd floor of Landmark Center, this museum in downtown St. Paul is open from noon to 4 PM Sunday through Friday. Upon entering one is immediately greeted by the tornado of instruments, an impressive towering structure of real instruments piled on top of one another. The guide, when asked if any had ever fallen off, assured us, no.

Children will find several hands-on related musical activities at the museum. At the Keyboards Expand, Music Evolves exhibit in the first location rooms, touching the panel buttons by the instrument pictured produced how it sounds when playing "Twinkle, Twinkle Little Star" or a composition from the period of its invention.

The second location rooms is a short walk down the hall to the Gamelan Music Room with its collection of gongs, kettles and tuned metal bars. First, view the video showing an orchestra performing with these unique Indonesian instruments. Then with assistance from a guide, children can use a padded hammer (gamelan) to strike the gongs which vary in size. The bigger the gong, the greater the vibration.

The final activity is the Try It! Invent an Instrument in the adjacent Musical Experimentation Room. Here children using the tracing paper and pencil provided can trace instrument images found on the table or walls to create their own idea of a musical instrument. Judging by the finished creations on display, the inventors took this challenge seriously. Although admission is free, donations are welcome.

*SCIENCE MUSEUM OF MINNESOTA (SMM)

120 W. Kellogg Blvd.
St. Paul, 55102

651-221-9444
www.smm.org

Think of our Science Museum of Minnesota as an upside down building. The main entrance on Kellogg Blvd. is the Lobby or Level 5. Level 5 is also the entrance to the Omni Theater, located on both Level 5 and Level 6. Levels 4 through 1 are down.

Pick up upon entering a Map & Guide brochure. It identifies the permanent exhibits on each level and special attractions locations during your visit. Look for a kiosk located near the stairways. The daily schedule of Science Live Performances and descriptions of Science Lives Shows are listed here.

Each visit to SMM for us includes a visit to Iggy, the steel nail-scaled iguana created by Nicholas Swearer in 1974-1977. We first met Iggy when he greeted visitors at the SMM entrance when located on 10th and Exchange. Now we find him by wandering down to Level 2 where he welcomes visitors outside the Education entrance on Eagle and Chestnut. Children still cannot climb on him, but that's still O.K. because we feel he still is here to encourage children to interact with most of the exhibits and ask lots of questions.

On Level 3 is another favorite, the Dinosaurs and Fossils Gallery. Push a button to highlight the scar on the 70 million year-old triceratops dinosaur skeleton and read how the scar is thought to have come about!

The Big Back Yard accessible via exhibit elevator to Level 1 is a seasonal outdoor gallery. When open, the Prairie Maze, Science House and Panning for Gems activity can be visited for free with museum admission. The 9 hole mini-golf activity has an additional fee of from $3 to $4.50.

As so many varied learning experiences and activities for children on all levels and for all ages are offered, it is best to connect with the SMM via calling or visiting the website for schedules of tours, events, attractions, classes, school and group programs.

The museum hours vary seasonally. So it is best to check on hours before going by calling or by website. Exhibit admission is $11 for adults and $8.50 for seniors and children 4 to 12. Memberships are available which reduce admissions and class fees. Visit the website or call 651-221-9409 for membership information.

*SEA LIFE MINNESOTA AQUARIUM
Mall of America (MOA) East Entrance Level One
120 E. Broadway
Interstate 494 & Hwy. 77
Bloomington, 55425

952-883-0202 (infoline)
1-866-823-9317
www.visitsealife.com/minnesota

Awarded the World's Best Shark Encounter by the Discovery Channel, the aquarium is a showcase for over 10,000 aquatic creatures including Brutus, a very large snapping turtle. When purchasing tickets, pickup the Talk & Feeds Timetable flyer for the daily schedule of event times and locations. Could be "Ray Tank Talk" is one.

Upon entering the aquarium, the Ray Lagoon with its walk-over platform for better viewing has many sting rays. Continuing along children will find the touch pools with its many horseshoe crabs and chocolate chip sea stars.

Still our favorite, the curved glass underwater Ocean Tunnel contains fish of all sizes swimming above and on both sides as you walk through it. Most interesting is to look up as a large fish swims above.

The Koi Pond near the end is an unusual exhibit. The fish look like giant goldfish. As we watched, we wondered what was causing their swimming frenzy. Were they hungry? Were they playing? Was this normal behavior?

At the Exit, look for the small Shark Nursery aquarium in the Diagnostic Lab window. In answer to the question "How many baby sharks can you find?" our group answer was 5 after we discovered the 3 hidden in the little shark house.

Hours are most days 10 AM to 7:30 PM except Sunday's 6:30 PM closing. But call or check the website for current changes. Admission prices are from $14.99 to $19.99. Children under 2 are free. Group rates are available for 10 people or more. Contact Group Sales (952-853-0612) in advance for group reservations.

*SIBLEY HOUSE HISTORICAL SITE
Minnesota Historical Society (MHS)
1357 Sibley Memorial Hwy. near State Hwy. 55
Mendota, 55150

651-452-1596
www.mnhs/org/places/sites/shs

This is the home of the first governor of Minnesota. The house was recently refurbished in the period of the late 1830s to late 1850s. Built in 1836 for Henry Hastings Sibley, who was also a prominent fur trader and military leader, the house was the center of pioneer life. The Faribault House, located on the Sibley site, can be visited, too. It also has been restored and houses a fine collection of North American artifacts including pipes, beadwork and clothing items. On the southeast corner of the Sibley property is the Hypolite du Puis House reception center. Here special events are held.

The Sibley House is open Saturday from 10 AM to 4 PM and Sunday from 12:30 PM to 4 PM from Memorial Day through Labor Day. Admission is $6 for adults, $5 for seniors and $4 for children ages 6 through 17. Children 5 and under are admitted free. Admission includes visits to the Sibley and Faribault Houses as well as the Sibley Cold Store, a restored fur trading post also on the grounds. Tours are offered with the last one beginning at 3 PM. During the fall and spring months, field trips, group and educational tours can also be arranged through reservations.

Note: Special weekend events and programs are offered in season. Children's Day includes playing games and doing activities popular during the mid-19th century. Fur Trade Rendezvous involves activities in the Cold Store. Call to inquire or visit the website about the upcoming events.

*SIERRA CLUB NORTH STAR CHAPTER
2327 E. Franklin Ave. Suite 1
Minneapolis, 55406

612-455-2128 (infoline)
www.northstar.sierraclub.org

The Sierra Club North Star Chapter has many outings some of which families would enjoy. Outing leaders are available to answer questions about the skill levels needed to participate in the activities. Families interested in more information should contact the club office or visit the website and select the option Get Outdoors.

The club published the North Star Journal newsletter with paper copies mailed to members. It is also available on the website at News.

SPRINGBROOK NATURE CENTER
Fridley Recreation & Natural Resources Dept.
100 85th Ave. N.
Fridley, 55432

763-572-3588
www.springbrooknaturecenter.org

Springbrook Nature Center is located on 127 acres of park land only a half mile west of Northtown Mall on 85th Ave. N. The Interpretive Center houses many exhibits and is the center from which many of their environmental and outdoor education programs originate. The center's Fall/Winter weekday hours are Monday to Friday from 9 AM to 5 PM. The Spring/Summer weekday hours are Monday to Friday from 9 AM to 9 PM. Year around the weekend hours are Saturday from 9 AM to 5 PM and Sunday noon to 4 PM. The 3 miles of hiking trails are open from 5 AM to 10 PM daily.

Seasonal newsletters listing the center's special events, programs and nature/science camps are available. I suggest stopping by the center for one as we did recently on a Saturday morning. At our visit during the Animal Feeding program, we met Tank, the 25 year old snapping turtle, an albino corn snake and saw through the exhibit room's window, a visiting hawk sitting on a tree limb. The Spring Fling and Pumpkin Night in the Park are popular seasonal events. And scout programs and birthday parties are choices, also. Many activities are free. Others have a small program fees, like the $3 per visit for Playful Polliwogs program on Tuesdays. The website lists them all.

*STAGES THEATRE COMPANY
Hopkins Center for the Arts
1111 Mainstreet
Hopkins, 55343

952-979-1111 (infoline)
www.stagestheatre.org

Children age 4 and up will enjoy the plays put on by this theatre company with the motto, Our World Is Magical. At least 6 different plays are presented throughout their magical theatrical season. Performances have included Princess Academy and Giggle, Giggle, Quack among other popular stories. Admission is $15 for adults and $12 for seniors and children ages 5 to 17. Group rates are available. The plays are performed Wednesdays through Sundays and an occasional Monday.

Many workshops and classes in acting are offered, also. They are organized into age groupings of 4 to 6, 7 to 13 and 14 and up. Tuition for workshops for children in the age group of 4 to 6 begin at $110. For the availability of scholarships and all the details on the many offerings, visit the website or call.

*STEAMBOAT MINNEHAHA
Museum of Lake Minnetonka (MLM)
P.O. Box 178
Excelsior, 55331

952-474-2115
www.steamboatminnehaha.org

Steamboats provided Twin City citizens with transportation across Lake Minnetonka from 1906 to 1926. The Minnehaha, scuttled in 1926, was raised from the lake in 1980 and completely restored by 1996.

Today, from Memorial Day through Labor Day on Saturdays, Sundays and holidays, the Minnehaha provides rides once again on Lake Minnetonka. The Round Trip Excelsior/Wayzata cruise of about 1 hour each way departs from Excelsior City Dock at 10:20 AM and returns from Wayzata City Dock at 1:30 PM. Shorter trips of 45 minutes to 1 hour, the Lake Cruises, depart from either Wayzata or Excelsior from 11:30 AM to 5:30 PM and may be just right for the family with younger children. Fares are $10 for adults and $5 for seniors and children ages 12 and under. Children have been known to be invited to steer the boat. For location directions, current schedules and reservation information call or visit the website.

*STEPPINGSTONE THEATRE
55 Victoria St. N.
St. Paul, 55104

651-225-9265
www.steppingstonetheatre.org

The theater strives to help develop self-esteem, confidence, leadership skills and creativity in children through learning performance arts. It also has the goal of educating its audience through the kinds of plays it performs each season.

The performers are children of ages 10 to 19. They have been selected from many diverse cultural backgrounds through open auditions. The plays are held year around and are varied in kind. They have included a musical featuring African-American dance and their traditional holiday show, The Best Christmas Pageant Ever. Tickets are $14 for adults and

$10 for seniors and children with group discounts available. During the production period, public performances are usually Friday and Saturday evenings at 7 PM and Sunday afternoons at 3 PM. However, it is best to call or visit the website for each play's schedule.

Note: School groups are encouraged to attend the plays. School performances are scheduled for Wednesday through Friday at 10 AM and 12 PM. Request study guides when making reservations. The guides help prepare for what will be seen and then talked about after the performance.

*JOHN H. STEVENS HOUSE HISTORIC MUSEUM
4901 Minnehaha Ave. S.
Minneapolis, 55417

612-722-2220
www.johnhstevenshouse.org

Located in Minnehaha Falls Park, the Stevens house, the little white house, not the large yellow one, is on the site of the birthplace of Minneapolis. It is now restored to its original 1849-1850 appearance by the Junior League of Minneapolis and the Minneapolis Park & Recreation Board. Today, it is interpretive museum. Visitors will learn that it was also the first school house when the parlor became a classroom.

Weekdays, children in grade 3 and up in group tours can experience educational activities planned for them through reservations scheduled at least 2 weeks in advance. Children, on a visit today, will find it interesting to learn that school children in 1896 saved the house by pulling it with ropes to the park from its downtown location.

The hours for regular scheduled tours are noon to 4 PM Sundays and Holidays from Memorial Day through Labor Day. Donations of $3 for adults and $1 for ages 17 and under are accepted. At other times, a group interested in a tour should contact the tour coordinator for arrangements at least 2 weeks in advance.

Note: Monthly summer events are held on the lawn outside the house. These are free to the public. Click on the calendar on the website for dates and the special activities planned for these events.

STORYTIMES
Most libraries and many bookstores in the Twin Cities have regularly scheduled storytime programs for children. Besides Saturdays, programs may be held after school for the older child, weekdays for the preschool and

toddler ages and evenings for children who can't attend during the day. Besides introducing books and other reading related activities, the librarians and storytellers like to present reading as a joyful, magical time. Contact the nearest library or ask at a children's bookstore about days and times.

TAMARACK NATURE CENTER
Ramsey County Parks & Recreation Dept.
Bald Eagle & Otter Lakes Regional Park
5287 Otter Lake Rd.
White Bear Township, 55110

651-407-5350
www.co.ramsey.mn.us/parks/tamarack

This 320-acre preserve in White Bear Township has naturalists who will lead groups on hiking tours of the 3.5 miles of trails. Nature classes on subjects such as pond life, bird banding and animal tracking are offered to the public. Fees for programs range from free to $16. Schools and community groups can arrange for programs such as apple cider making and migration mysteries through advance arrangements. Day camps are offered in summer with fees ranging from $25 to $190.

The hiking trails are open 1/2 hour before sunrise to 1/2 hour after sunset. A naturalist is present at the nature center most hours which are 8:30 AM to 4:30 PM Monday through Friday, 9 AM to 5 PM Saturday and noon to 5 PM on Sunday.

Note: Birthday parties can be held at the center with choices beginning at $60. Reservations in advance are necessary. For all the details, contact the center or visit the website.

*THOMAS C. SAVAGE VISITOR CENTER
101 Snelling Lake Rd. at State Hwy. 5 & Post Rd.
St. Paul, 55111

612-725-2724
www.dnr.state.mn.us/parks

Located within Fort Snelling State Park, the center offers programs throughout the year for families, groups and individuals interested in nature studies. One of the programs is the Annual Bluebird Recovery Workshop that includes a film, discussion on how to get started and information on bluebird houses. School and other groups by appointment can arrange for a group program at the center. A schedule of all their programs can be requested. There can be a small supplies fee for some programs.

The center is open to the public every day 8 AM to 4 PM. A daily State Park grounds entry fee of $5 is charged for each vehicle. An annual pass for all Minnesota state parks is $25. For sanctioned school groups of kindergarten age through grade 12, the entry fee is waived.

*THREE RIVERS PARK DISTRICT
Park District Headquarters
3000 Xenium Lane N.
Plymouth, 55441

763-559-9000 (infoline)
www.threeriverspark.org

Three Rivers Park offers many indoor and outdoor activities for families. Explore the world of squirrels, observe birds migrating south for the winter, or follow animal tracks on snowshoes. Depending on the time of year, children can participate in these programs and many others. For a copy of Discoveries, the Park publication listing the activities and programs planned for each season of the year, call 763-559-9000. Or select News on the website to stay informed of what's newsworthy at Three Rivers.

Visit Three Rivers Park website and select Activities & Events for a listing of all the options. It should be noted that many of the Three Rivers activities are free. For those with daily fee passes or activity fees, purchasing is available online, onsite or by telephone. For those requiring reservations, the availability to do so is online or by calling 763-559-6700.

The park Nature & Interpretive Centers are:

Eastman Nature Ctr., Elm Creek Park, Dayton, 55369 (763-694-7700)
Lowry Nature Ctr., Carver Park, Victoria, 55386 (763-694-7650)
Richardson Nature Ctr., Hyland Lake Park, Bloomington, 55438
    (763-694-7676)
Kroening Interpretive Ctr., N. Mississippi Park, Brooklyn Ctr., 55430
    (763-694-7693)
Silverwood Park, St. Anthony Village, 55421 (763-694-7707)

The Play Area at Hyland Lake Park Reserve is fondly known by visitors as chutes and ladders. Children and parents know it as lots of fun because of all the slides and ladders there. The longest slide is 50 feet and the shortest is 3 feet in the toddler playground. An added attraction, the misters, are especially cooling for a run through on hot summer days. The play area is open dawn until dust. The park location is 10145 E. Bush Lake Rd., Bloomington. Within the park, the Play Area is located south and west of the Hyland Ski & Snowboard area (763-694-7800).

Elm Creek Park Reserve in Dayton has a swimming pond for summer enjoyment and tubing hill, snowboarding, down hill and cross country skiing for winter enjoyment. Daily passes are $3 for swimming and $12 for tubing with skiing $4 to $25. Contact the park reserve's Visitor Center at 763-694-7894 for details.

Note: The Minnesota, Mississippi, and Crow rivers, all of which abut or run through one or more of the parks, give the district its name.

*TOUCH & SEE ROOM
Bell Museum of Natural History
University of Minnesota, Minneapolis Campus
10 Church St.
University Ave. & 17th Ave. S. E.
Minneapolis, 55455

612-624-7083 (infoline)
www.bellmuseum.org/touchandsee.html

In this special room everything is at child height and almost everything can be handled. There are skeletons, skins, bones and other animal parts for children to touch and examine. There are live snakes that can be handled with friendly staff supervision. There are even mounted antlers for children to try on for size. A corner of the room is set aside with large beanbag pillows and natural history books for children to read. The room is open Tuesday through Friday from 9 AM to 5 PM, Saturday from 10 AM to 5 PM and Sundays from noon to 5 PM. Admission to the Bell Museum is $5 for adults and $3 for children ages three to 16 and seniors except on Sundays when admission is free. No additional fees are charged for entering this special room.

TPT, INC.
172 E. 4th St.
St. Paul, 55101

651-222-1717
www.tpt.org

From November through April, tours for families with children of any age are offered at TPT (Twin Cities Public Television). The 30-minute tour takes visitors into the studio and control rooms to see and hear about all the technical operations necessary to run the station.

Tours are given the first Saturday of the month beginning at 10 AM with the last tour starting at 11:30 AM. No reservations needed.

*TRAIN RIDES AT OSCEOLA
Osceola & St. Croix Valley Railway (OSCVRY)
PO Box 176
114 Depot Rd.
Osceola, WI 54020

1-715-755-3570 (Osceola)
www.trainride.org

Beginning in May and continuing through October and only a short 1 hour drive from the Twin Cities, we can once again experience a passenger train ride in Osceola, WI. On weekends and holidays, the diesel passenger trains travel on routes to Marine on the St. Croix, MN and Dresser, WI. All trains depart from the historic former Soo Line Depot on Depot Road and Hwy. 35 in Osceola. The rides are 90 minutes round trip for a family fare of $45 for the Marine on the St. Croix trip. The 50 minutes round trip family fare is $25 for the Dresser trip. Call or visit the website for schedules and other fare options including school group rates, directions, reservation details and information on special events like the Pumpkin Express Train and Fall Leaf Viewing trips.

Note: The Minnesota Transportation Museum (MTM), a volunteer organization, located in St. Paul (651-228-0263) owns and operates OSCVRY.

*TRAIN CITY MODEL RAILROAD MUSEUM (TCMRM)
Bandana Square Building
1021 Bandana Blvd. E., Suite 222
St. Paul, 55108

651-647-9628
www.tcmrm.org

Climb the stairs to the 2nd floor location for a wonderful exhibit of trains, trolleys and buildings presenting railroading in the United States during the 1930s, 1940s and 1950s. It includes reproductions of Twin Cities scenes such as the Northern Pacific Como shops (now Bandana Square) and the St. Anthony Falls Milling District. In 3,500 square feet of space two double track main lines, one for passenger trains and one for freight, form the layout for the O-scale model trains (one-quarter inch to the foot). Visiting hours are Tuesday through Thursday from 11 AM to 3 PM, Friday from 11 AM to 5 PM, Saturday from 10 AM to 5 PM and Sunday from noon to 5 PM. The museum's members, all volunteers, can be seen working on the exhibit Tuesday and Thursday evenings from 7 to 8:30. Especially nice for children is a railing with platforms which surrounds the layout. Children can stand on the platforms to see even better the trains and trolleys go by on the tracks.

The admission fee is $6 for ages 5 and older. Children under 5 are free.

Note: The fee includes admission for a visit to the new Toy Train Division begun in 2008 when an extensive collection of Lionel trains and equipment was donated to TCMRM. Open to the public Saturday from 10 AM to 5 PM and Sunday from 12 PM to 5 PM, miniature train collections, many of them works-in-progress, are located in the historic 1880's Chimney's Building just North of Bandana Square. Also here is where children can have fun building their own toy train at the Thomas the Tank Engine layout.

*TWINS BASEBALL
Target Field
1 Twins Way
Minneapolis, 55414

612-33-TWINS (infoline)
1-800-33-TWINS
www.twinsbaseball.com

The Minnesota Twins, World Series Champions of 1987 and 1991, play ball from April to October in downtown Minneapolis at the new Target Field. Twins Poster Schedules, Bat, Cap and other special promotional days are held throughout the season to encourage families to attend a ball game. Single ticket prices range from $12 to $85. Each season the Twins also offer special adult and child value deal promotions that might include a coupon for a food item.

In late January, **TwinsFest** is held Friday through Sunday at a Twin City location. It, too, is a family event. The Twins organization provides opportunities to meet current and past players and coaches, participate in fun baseball skills activities, etc. Tickets range from $5 to $15. This event benefits the Minnesota Twins Community Fund that supports youth baseball and softball programs and is always well attended.

So let's all go to a ball game where fun is part of the game!

Note: During the baseball season, the Twins organization holds free baseball youth clinics for boys and girls ages 6 to 16. These sessions focus on skills of fielding, hitting, throwing and base running. Contact 612-33-TWINS for locations and more information. Or use the website **www.playballminnesota.com** and select LATEST NEWS to locate the baseball and softball contacts for these youth programs closest to home in your area.

*UNIVERSITY OF MINNESOTA
Youth & Community Programs
104 St. Paul Campus Gymnasium
1536 N. Cleveland Ave.
St. Paul, 55108

612-625-2242
www.recsports.umn.edu/youth

Throughout the year, the U's Department of Recreational Sports offers youth programs for children ages 5 to 15. They include summer day camps and birthday parties.

The summer camps are week-long themed programs held from mid-June through August. Choices including sports, art, science, music, etc. All camps include swim-time in the indoor pool, indoor rock climbing and lots of outdoor play activities. The camps are Monday through Friday from 7:30 AM to 5:30 PM with nearby free check-in and check-out parking. Program fees begin at $194 and up per week with registration available online beginning in February. As each themed camp has a 13 maximum size, early enrollment is encouraged.

Birthday parties for up to 10 and of ages 5 to 15 can be scheduled for Saturday and Sunday afternoons from September through May and once a month during the summer months. They too have themes. Choose from indoor rock climbing, swimming and science. Costs begin at $140 and up. Details including options for adding goodies are available at the website.

Call and request the brochures that describe all the details including costs, age limitations, dates and registration procedures. Information about the programs can also be found on the websites.

Note: Additional programs offered by the U's Department of Recreational Sports include Learn to Swim **www.recsports.umn.edu/aquatics** (612-625-3794) for ages 6 months and up and School of Golf lessons **www.recsports.umn.edu/golf** (612-627-4000) for all ages and abilities. Visit websites or call for details.

UPPER ST. ANTHONY'S FALLS LOCK & DAM
Army Corps of Engineers
1 Portland Ave.
Minneapolis, 55401

1-877-552-1416
www.mvp.usace.army.mil

Now only prebooked tours are available. They can be scheduled from 10 AM to 6 PM during the navigation season, which usually begins in May and continues into October. Children, who must be accompanied by an adult, will find viewing the locks below most interesting, and with luck may see a boat come through.

To schedule a tour e-mail **dam.tours@usace.army.mil** or call beginning in mid-April. Information requested includes contact and how to reach, size and age of tour and date and time desired.

Note: Lock & Dam No. 1, a newly discovered yet long-time existing lock & dam, also known as the Ford Dam, does have a public access observation deck. Open the end of May through October, its at 5000 W. River Road, south of Ford Bridge. Look for signage. Parking is limited. Call 612-724-2971 in April for updates.

*VALLEYFAIR FAMILY AMUSEMENT PARK
One Valleyfair Drive
State Hwy. 101
Shakopee, 55379

952-445-7600 or 952-445-6500 (infoline)
1-800-386-7433
www.valleyfair.com

"For the Biggest Family Day Around" visit the delightful family amusement park, Valleyfair. Located on 90 acres of land 3 miles east of Shakopee, it is open 7 days a week from mid-May through Labor Day and then weekends in September and October. Both children and adults will find this an enjoyable and sparkling clean entertaining place to visit. Plan at least 6 hours to see and do it all.

Don't miss driving the antique autos and riding on the authentic 1925 carousel which was originally built for the Excelsior Minnesota Amusement Park. These are rides that can be enjoyed by all ages. Other favorites are the bumper cars and the family roller coaster ride, Mad Mouse. For the adventurous family, the Wave is particularly nice on a hot day as you ride down the water-filled chute and get wet. The Corkscrew is a head-over-heels experience for the brave.

There are many activity areas planned especially for children of 54 inches or shorter. They include the Corkscrew Totspot for the very young with its Kiddie Carousel, Moon Buggies and Kiddie U-Turn racing car rides. **Planet Snoopy**, new in 2011, has 20 rides and attractions for children and adults to enjoy. On a recent visit Sally's Swing Set, Snoopy's Junction train ride and Lucy's Rockin Tug, with twists and motions of being caught in a storm were fun for all family members. Also in Snoopy's location, the Peanuts Playhouse is an indoor building. In it are hundreds of soft, pastel colored balls for imaginative play with Cannon Blasters, giant Ball Bagger vacuum upper and other oversized giant toys including a pulley system for hoisting bags of balls to the playhouse's upper deck level.

Note: For safety precautions, all rides have height requirements and thrill ratings posted at each ride's entrance. The Valleyfair Park Map & Guide received upon entrance has this information also.

Finally, step aboard the Minnesota River Valley Railroad for a train ride around the park grounds.

A single day general admission to the park is $39.99 for ages 3 to 61. Children 3 years and older and less than 48 inches tall and seniors 62 and older are admitted for $9.99. The admission fee includes access to all 75 plus rides and shows. Parking is $10. Valleyfair hours are 10 AM to varying closing times of 6 to 12 PM depending on the day of the week and season of the year. Call or check the website.

Soak City Waterpark, located on the Valleyfair grounds, is a special attraction with no additional admission fee charged for entrance and enjoyment. Tubes are available to ride down long, wet chutes of water. Bring your own bathing suits and towels. Lockers are available for a partial refundable fee. This is loads of fun judging by the many smiling faces seen the day we visited.

VISION OF PEACE
St. Paul City Hall/Ramsey County Court House
Memorial Hall
15 W. Kellogg Blvd.
St. Paul, 55102

Carl Milles, the well-known sculptor, created this work of art from the concept of Native Americans gathering in council to smoke their sacred pipes. Rising from the smoke of the pipe, Milles envisioned a "god of peace" statue which he sculpted holding a sacred pipe and extending a hand in friendship.

Children seem in awe of this huge, 36-foot tall statue when they first view it. Sculpted from white Mexican onyx and weighing 60 tons, it rotates very slowly 132 degrees. The building is open from 8 AM to 4:30 PM Monday through Friday. Group tours can be arranged by calling 651-266-8002. There are no group size or age limitations.

Note: An excellent, informative self-guided free tour flyer is also available at the desk on the 1st floor next to the elevator or in Room 250. It contains lots of interesting details about the Concourse Level, i.e. basement. And do as it suggests…ask the guard to start the glass mural's light show.

*WALKER ART CENTER
1750 Hennepin Ave.
Minneapolis, 55403

612-375-7600 (infoline)
http://learn.walkerart.org

Many programs for children are offered throughout the year at Walker Art Center. An expansion to the building with a new wing in 2005 added 2 interactive education tools, a dolphin with artificial intelligence and an arcade-like audio video fractoid machine. To interact with these alone are worth a visit.

Free First Saturdays is a full day of family art fun for all ages. Held on the first Saturday of the month from 10 AM to 3 PM, admission to the center is free for everyone this day. The family activities planned have a different theme for each month. There is always a hands-on art activity. Other happenings could include a film, art tour, dance performance and storytelling.

Arty Pants: Your Tuesday Playdate is for children ages 3 to 5 and requires an accompanying adult. Appropriate art projects, films, gallery activities and storytimes are planned for this age group. The playdates are from 11 AM to 1 PM on the 2nd and 4th Tuesday of each month The adult attendee pays the museum admission fee but the children attendees are free.

Additional details on each of these programs can be obtained on the website **www.walkerart.org** from the LEARN option. Then select KIDS & FAMILIES and scroll through At the Walker.

The Walker offers other programs including group tours. To schedule a tour, call 612-375-7609 during the hours 10 AM to 5 PM Monday through Friday or visit the websites at anytime.

The art center hours are Tuesday through Sundays from 11 AM to 5 PM except on Thursday when open until 9 PM. It is closed on Monday. Admission is $10 for adults, $8 for seniors and $6 for students. Youth 18 and under are free. Gallery admission to the Walker is free for everyone Thursday evenings from 5 PM to 9 PM.

*WARNER NATURE CENTER
15375 Norell Ave. N.
Marine-on-St. Croix, 55047

651-433-2427 (infoline)
www.warnernaturecenter.ORG

The center located in the St. Croix Valley operates in partnership with the Science Museum of Minnesota. Most of the programs are planned for children in elementary grades and up. However, public events include family programs for children as young as two.

Explore. Educate. Connect.

Seasonal education and recreation classes are offered all year around. There's snowshoeing, canoeing, spring maple syruping and stargazing to list a few. Some programs require preregistration. Some are free. Others have fees beginning at $5 for ages 13 and older and $3 and up for children ages 3 to 12.

For current and upcoming descriptions of the many family programs, the website has information at the Public Program option. As an alternative, one can contact the center Monday through Friday from 8 AM to 4 PM and inquire about receiving a Public Program Calendar.

Note: Mothers and dads, scout leaders, educators and others are encourages to arrange visits as part of a school science program or badge requirement or church school experience. Also birthday party packages and summer camp programs are available.

*WAY-COOL COOKING SCHOOL
16544 W. 78th St.
Eden Prairie, 55344

952-949-6799
www.waycoolcookingschool.com

The school offers lots of choices for children from ages 4 and up. With emphasis on fun and healthy eating, the complete listing of cooking classes and events (including some for adults) is on their website. Fees for classes begin at $45 and up per child. Birthday party packages start at $285.

At a class making spaghetti sauce, the children learned that by crushing the Italian seasonings before adding releases their oils resulting in a sauce that's "better than in the can" according to one small chef's taste test. The class went on to make cheesy garlic bread and smoothies in a bag. And then they enjoyed it all for lunch.

With humor added to the informative teaching and with many helpers, groups of even 50 can be accommodated at this lively, yet well organized school.

Note: A second Way-Cool Cooking School is located in the Woodbury Kowalski's Market, 8505 Valley Creek Rd, 55125. Contact 952-949-6799 for classes at this location.

WCCO TELEVISION STUDIOS
Communications Dept.
90 S. 11th St.
Minneapolis, 55403

612-339-4444
www.wcco.com

Children 10 and older can tour the station. Stops include the air control room, newsroom, weather center and news studio. Tours are scheduled Tuesday and Thursday at 10 AM and 2 PM. The tours last about 30 to 45 minutes with advance reservations needed. Groups of 5 to 15 can be accommodated.

Note: The newsroom set is visible through glass windows facing the Nicollet Mall sidewalk. Stop by and look in.

WESTWOOD HILLS NATURE CENTER
8300 W. Franklin Ave.
St. Louis Park, 55426

952-924-2544
www.stlouispark.org/parks-rec/westwood-hills-nature-center.html

More than 3 miles of paved and woodchip trails wind through a marsh at this 160 acre environmental center. There is a quarter mile floating board-walk crossing a lake for walkers, hikers and explorers to enjoy. The center is owned and operated by the City of St. Louis Park. The Interpretative Center building is open from 8 AM to 4:30 PM weekdays year around and on weekends from noon to 5 PM February through November.

Special Family Programs are held on a regular basis throughout the year. There is maple syruping in the spring and pond life in summer and others which change from time to time. Naturalist-led tours can be scheduled for family groups, school groups and other youth groups, too. A few of the programs have a small fee.

The center has a Wild Flower Trail that is a quarter mile accessible paved trail leading through wild flower fields and past a frog pond...croak, croak. Look for the honeybee apiary along the way. And the bird watching con-tinues to be excellent at the Westwood Hills Nature Center according to the center's naturalists. Trail hours are dawn to dusk year around.

Something new is happening here everyday. To be put on a mailing to receive the center's seasonal listing of programs, contact them or visit the website to see the seasonal listings.

Note: Birthday parties for ages 4 and up can be scheduled for Saturday and Sunday afternoons with advance reservations a must. For party time, the center provides a room, a brief introduction to the area and a naturalist-led hike and other activities. The resident fee is $85 and non-resident $90 for the reserved party. The birthday treats are supplied by the party givers.

WILD RUMPUS
Books for Young Readers
2720 W. 43rd St.
Minneapolis, 55410

612-920-5005
www.wildrumpusbooks.com

This children's bookstore has special Saturday events that begin at 1 PM and end when "you say WHEN!" Past events have included a sheepshearer, a forensic entomologist and a rodeo star. Some events need reservations. Contact Wild Rumpus for event information or visit the website and look for Upcoming Wild Times. While on the website, one can also sign up to receive their newsletter announcing the upcoming events. And what's unique? Shelves of recycled books for 25 cents to $1 a book. And what's weird? Look for the floor grate to see a rat living beneath the floorboards.

WOOD LAKE NATURE CENTER
Richfield Park & Recreation Dept.
6710 Lake Shore Dr.
Richfield, 55423

612-861-9365
www.woodlakenaturecenter.org/

Wood Lake Nature Center is an exciting place for children and adults to explore together. Saturday and Sunday Specials are especially planned for families and individuals. All programs are offered on a no-reservations, first come basis and most do have space limitations. Some are free to all. Others are free for member attendees with non-members paying a small fee of $3 to $5. These special activities range from astronomy to whole earth cookery. Programs on bird house building and honey extraction have also been offered. For more detailed information on all their events, programs, classes, activities and day/summer camps, contact the center to request the seasonal flyer or visit the website. Also available at the center are self-guiding materials that include a trail map and bird list.

Except for holidays, the center is open all year. The building hours are from Monday through Saturday 8:30 AM to 5 PM and Sunday noon to 5 PM. The park grounds hours are from 5 AM to 11 PM.

WORLD WAR II AVIATION MUSEUM
Commemorative Air Force (CAF)
Hangar #3 Fleming Field
310 Airport Rd.
South St. Paul, 55075

651-455-6942
www.cafmn.org

The Commemorative Air Force Minnesota Wing museum is open for free public visits on Wednesday and Saturdays between 10 AM and 5 PM. In the museum, one will see displays and aircraft restoration activities. As the museum is operated by CAF volunteers, it is best to call before going.

Scouts, school groups and other groups of any age can tour the aircraft restoration activity at other times. It is very important to call ahead of time for reservations for the tour.

Note: Visit the website to learn about the availability of a ride on the Miss Mitchell, a World War II B-25 bomber.

XCEL ENERGY
Public Safety Demonstrations
Corporate Headquarters
414 Nicollet Mall
Minneapolis, 55401

612-330-5500
1-800-828-6788

The Safety Demonstrations given by retired Xcel/NSP employees are very powerful. The presenter brings a demonstration kit from which he or she then sets up situations showing how to safely act around power lines. They show what to do if in a car near a downed power line and talk about kite flying near power lines. The program, which lasts from 45 minutes to an hour, is for school, scout and other groups of children of 3rd grade age and older. Call between 8 AM and 4 PM weekdays and ask for the Public Safety Department to arrange for this unique visit. It is best to schedule at least 2 weeks in advance. And be prepared to be asked for "what state?"

Note: The Xcel Energy Bird Cam on their website has a link to bird cams located in Colorado, Iowa and Minnesota. Also **www.birdcam. xcelenergy.com** is a direct link to the Raptor Resource Project. In the spring, this is a fun and educational way to monitor the activity of a growing peregrine falcon family as well as the nesting activities of an owl, kestrel, osprey and bald eagle.

*YMCA OF GREATER ST. PAUL & YMCA OF METROPOLITAN MINNEAPOLIS
www.ymcatwincities.org

Family, preschool and youth classes and programs are offered at most of the Y locations listed. Swimming, gymnastics, day camps, ballet, karate and skateboarding are just some of the many to choose from. Contact any of the Y's to inquire about their current classes, dates, fees and special events or stop by to pick up a descriptive brochure. The website is useful, too.

Kids Stuff is a drop-in center for children ages 6 weeks to 10 years. Activities are planned that may include games, storytelling, arts and crafts and free play. The Y describes it as "a special place that kids can call their own" while Mom and Dad get some exercise time, too. Children of members are free for up to 2 hours per day. The fee for a guest child is $4 per hour. The Kids Stuff brochure available at each location contains all the guidelines for use of the drop-in center.

St. Paul area locations:

East: St. Paul, 875 Arcade, 55106 (651-771-8881)
Midway Family: St. Paul, 1761 University Ave., 55104 (651-646-4557)
Northeast: White Bear Lake, 2100 Orchard Lane, 55110 (651-777-8103)
Northwest: Shoreview, 3760 N. Lexington Ave., 55126 (651-483-2671)
South Family: West St. Paul, 150 Thompson Ave. E., 55118 (651-457-0048)
Southeast Area: Woodbury, 2175 Radio Dr., 55125 (651-731-9507)
Southwest Area: Eagan, 550 Opperman Dr., 55123 (651-456-9622)

Minneapolis area locations:

Blaisdell: Minneapolis, 3335 Blaisdell Ave. S., 55408 (612-827-5401)
**Minnesota Valley Family: Burnsville, 13850 Portland Ave. S., 55337
    (952-898-9622)**
Northwest: New Hope, 7601 42nd Ave. N., 55427 (763-535-4800)
Ridgedale: Minnetonka, 12301 Ridgedale Dr., 55305 (952-544-7708)
Southdale: Edina, 7355 York Ave. S., 55435 (952-835-2567)

Join one, join them all, with an adult one-month Metro Family membership for $112.

*YOUTH PERFORMANCE COMPANY (YPC)
3338 University Ave. SE
Minneapolis, 55414

612-623-9080 (infoline)
www.youthperformanceco.com

YPC presents 4 to 5 new stories each season. These are often familiar tales but done in original, often humorous ways. A Winnie the Pooh Christmas Tail and School House Rock Line have been performed. Serious plays have included Mean, an original play on the impact of bullying and MVP-The Jackie Robinson Story based on the life of this American hero. Most plays are recommended for children of age 7 or 8 and older with at least one during the season for all ages.

Performances are at the Howard Conn Fine Arts Center, 1900 Nicollet Ave. in Minneapolis, 55403 with free parking. Ticket prices are $12 for adults and $10 for seniors and children 18 and under. Ticket discounts are available for groups of 10 or more. Performances are usually Thursday through Sunday and are usually 10 AM and 12:30 PM weekdays and 2 PM and 7:30 PM on weekends. Visit the website or call for the current performance information.

Saturday and summer classes on theatre arts are offered for grades kindergarten through 12. Visit the website or contact YPC at 612-623-9180 ext. 102 for current class and cost information. For the summer workshops, children not only do the performing but they help write the script and music. Depending upon the play, they may get involved in making the costumes and sets, too.

*THE ZOO
13000 Zoo Blvd.
Apple Valley, 55124

952-431-9200 or 952-431-9500 (infoline)
1-800-366-7811
www.mnzoo.org

Minnesota Zoo visitors can discover and enjoy seeing more than 5,000 animals as well as thousands of plants in exhibits representing the natural habitats of the animals and birds. Several trips a year are needed to see and participate in all the activities offered by the zoo.

Upon entering the main building, check at the Guest Services Desk for a listing of the daily events. This could include times for animal feedings, special shows, tours and other announcements for the day. Then plan at least 4 hours of delightful discoveries. But don't miss out on seeing the dolphins, our favorites. Be sure to visit the penguin exhibit opened in 2011. And on a cold winter day, the Tropics Trail and Discovery Bay are especially pleasant for the lush, colorful vegetation.

Open during the warm weather months, the Wells Fargo Family Farm is where children can see and touch and experience life in a farm setting. In April, the Farm Babies return when chicks, piglets, and bunnies among other baby animals are present. On the grounds are a farmhouse, chicken house, swine barn, machine shed, goat and sheep barn and a grain elevator. When the Tractor Ride is operating, children can take a short trip on it.

A special attraction is the World of Birds with its several daily shows. On the Northern Trail of the zoo grounds is where the tigers, musk oxen, camels, wild horses and moose live outdoors all year. Walk through this area on the winding paths or ride through it on the monorail for $4.

The zoo opens at 9 AM with closing times of 4 PM or 6 PM depending upon the season of the year. Admission is $16 for adults, $10 for ages 3 through 12 and seniors and free for children 2 and under. Parking is $5. Group rates are available for 20 or more with 2 week advance reservations by calling the Group Sales office (952-431-9298). Zoo members are admitted free and park for free.

The zoo offers a number of programs to acquaint school age children with the animals. Through the School Scheduler (952-431-9218) arrangements can be made for school groups to come to the zoo for tours and programs. Or the Zoomobile can be scheduled (952-431-9228) to come to a school. For information about programs offered and fees for each of these options call or visit the zoo's website.

NOTES

DAY TRIPS

DAY TRIPS

These activities are located outside the Twin Cities. Plan at least a day's adventure for exploring.

*CHARLES A. LINDBERGH HISTORIC SITE
1620 Lindbergh Dr. S.
Little Falls, 56345

1-320-616-5421
www.mnhs.org/places/sites/lh

Located in Charles A. Lindbergh State Park, which is two miles south of Little Falls, the Lindbergh house is the boyhood home of Minnesota's famous aviator. The house was built in 1906 by his father and is kept as it was in 1927. Visitors can tour the house and the visitor's center. Special events are held on selected weekends throughout the summer.

The hours are Thursday through Saturday from 10 AM to 5 PM and noon to 5 PM on Sunday from Memorial Day weekend through Labor Day. Pre-arranged group tours can be arranged for visiting in May and September and October. Admission is from $5 to $7.

*COMSTOCK HOUSE
506 8th St. S.
Moorhead, 56560

1-218-233-4211
www.mnhs.org/places/sites/ch

On Hwy. 75 in Moorhead, a half mile north of the Hwy. I-94 exit, the Comstock House can be found. It is noted for being the home of two important Minnesotans, Solomon G. Comstock, a politician and businessman in this upper Red River Valley area for over 60 years and his daughter, Ada Comstock, the first dean of women at the University of Minnesota and then president of Radcliffe College from 1923 to 1943.

The house was built in 1882/83 and has been restored to portray the living conditions of that time. Guided tours tell the history of the Red River Valley and about the lives of the Comstocks.

Hours are from 1 to 4:30 PM weekends and from 5 to 8 PM Thursdays from the end of May through Labor Day. Other times can be arranged for groups through advance reservations. For guided tour hours, call or visit the website. Admission is from $4 to $6.

*FOREST HISTORY CENTER
2609 Cty. Rd. 76
Grand Rapids, 55744

1-218-327-4482
www.mnhs.org/places/sites/fhc

Located near Hwys. 169 and 2 West, the center shows with living history characters how the lumberjack lived at the turn of the century. This site features a logging camp with a fire tower, a floating cook shack used for log drives and a forest ranger cabin. There are over two miles of self-guided forest trails. The interactive museum exhibits include a state-of-the-art timber harvester simulator. This is a wonderful place to visit to hear the story of how people lived in the forests of Minnesota from ancient times to the present. Special events are held on some weekends.

From June through Labor Day, the logging camp and center are open from 11 AM to 4 PM Tuesday through Saturday. Winter hours are from September through May when the center and gift shop are open weekdays from 9 AM to 4 PM. Other times can be arranged for groups through advance reservations. Admission is from $5 to $8.

*FORT RIDGELY HISTORIC SITE
72404 Cty. Rd. 30
Fairfax, 55332

1-507-426-7888
www.mnhs.org/places/sites/fr

Located in Fort Ridgely State Park, which is seven miles south of Fairfax off Hwy. 4, Minnesota's third military post was closed and its buildings torn down after the U.S.-Dakota Indians Conflict of 1862. These building materials were then taken and used by the settlers to build their homes and barns. Today, a restored stone commissary is on the site. The visitor center has exhibits that help explain Fort Ridgely's history. Some remnants of the original buildings also remain for exploring. Special events are held on several summer weekends.

The site is open Memorial Day through Labor Day Friday and Saturday from 10 AM to 5 PM and Sunday from noon to 5 PM. And then with the same hours on weekends only through mid-October. Daily admission is $2 to $3. Also a state park vehicle permit is required.

*GREAT LAKES AQUARIUM (GLA)
353 Harbor Dr.
Duluth, 55802

1-218-740-FISH
1-877-866-3474
www.glaquarium.org

The Great Lakes Aquarium is more than an exhibit of fish in tanks. There are many exhibits of historical events that have taken place on or near Lake Superior, too. The aquarium, the only freshwater aquarium in the United States, opened the summer of 2000 and is still evolving. There are at least 70 species of freshwater fish as well as birds and ducks.

The Wall of Water at the lobby entrance is impressive. Look for the signage on the wall for an explanation of the many graphic symbols.

Also pick up the aquarium's daily schedule for the times and locations when special programs like Stingray Snacktime are held. On a recent visit a snake skin (without the snake) and turtle shell (without the turtle) were passed around for close-up looks during the Remarkable Reptiles program. With proper instructions for touching the live python snake given, all were invited to line-up to do so.

Children's favorites will include Zhoosh, the otter, in Otter Cove. Zhoosh means slide in Ojibway. The Water Table set-up for piloting small boats through locks is another favorite. At the Touch and See tank, a stingray can be stroked and a baby sturgeon petted. And piloting a virtual ore boat under the Aerial Lift Bridge was a serious experience for a 6 year old as she then continued to carefully steer between the piers and onto the Lake.

Hours are from 10 AM to 6 PM every day but Christmas. Admission is $14.50 for adults, $11.50 for seniors, $8.50 for children ages 3 to 16 and free for children under three. Parking is $4. To reach the aquarium, take Exit 256B from Hwy. I-35 to the large blue, green and red building near the waterfront.

Note: Special on-going events are held throughout the year. Birthday party packages with special rates for groups of 10 or more are available, too.

*HARKIN STORE HISTORIC SITE
PO Box 112
New Ulm, 56073

1-507-354-8666
www.mnhs.org/places/sites/hs

Located on Co. Hwy. 21 eight miles Northwest of New Ulm, this is a real 19th century general stores complete with many of the things left in the store when it closed in the 1870s due to the railroad bypassing the town. Clothing, medicine bottles and other items left on the shelves are still there. Costumed guides are on site to share stories of the era. Programs are every Sunday. Shop for period gifts!

From Memorial Day weekend through Labor Day the store is open from Tuesday through Sunday from 10 AM to 5 PM. During the months of May and September and October it is open Saturday and Sunday from 10 AM to 5 PM. Admission is $2 or $3.

*JEFFERS PETROGLYPHS HISTORIC SITE
27160 Cty. Rd. 2
Comfrey, 56019

1-507-628-5591
www.mnhs.org/places/sites/jp

Located three miles east of Hwy. 71 on Cottonwood Cty. Rd. 10, then one mile south on Cty. Rd. 2, this is the site of over 2000 carvings of human figures, weapons and animals made by North American Indians on ancient quartzite rocks. It is thought that some of the carvings date back to 3000 BC while others are as new as the 18th century. A visitor's center on the grounds contains an exhibit that helps to explain some of the carvings. It also describes the surrounding prairie ecology.

The hours for visiting are from 10 AM to 5 PM Monday and Thursday through Saturday 10 AM to 5 PM and noon to 5 PM Sunday from Memorial Day weekend through Labor Day. Check out the "For Kids" activities and program listings on the website. Also, a printable trail brochure is there as well. Admission is from $4 to $6.

*LAKE SUPERIOR & MISSISSIPPI RAILROAD (LSMR)
6930 Fremont St.
Duluth, 55807

1-218-624-7549
www.lsmrr.org

This train ride is a great discovery. For many years now, this train ride has been providing scenic trips along the St. Louis River on track built in 1870 to connect Duluth with the Twin Cities. During the 12 mile round trip, passengers may see bears, beavers, deer and many different birds like ducks, geese and herons. The ride can be described as a "nature walk on rails."

Operated since 1981 by a group of dedicated volunteers from the Lake Superior Transportation Club, the members are continually working on maintaining the vintage coach cars, a bright yellow locomotive and the open air flat green Safari Car.

Tickets are purchased at the white and blue Excursion Train booth where one can also purchase train souvenirs like whistles, engineer hats and paperweights make from 120 year-old rails. Tickets are $10.50 for adults and $6.50 for children ages 4 to 11. Departures are at 10:30 AM and 1:30 PM weekends from mid-June to early October. The ride is an hour and a half long.

To locate the railroad coming from the Twin Cities on Hwy. I-35 exit at 251A and make right turns on 63rd Ave. W and then Grand Ave. Look for their sign across from the Zoo. From Duluth on Hwy. I-35 exit left to Grand Ave. (251B) and go west to sign. Free parking is available in their large adjacent lot. Their mailing address is PO Box 16211, Duluth, 55816.

Note: The train can be chartered for birthday parties and other family fun events.

*LAKE SUPERIOR RAILROAD MUSEUM
The Depot
506 W. Michigan St.
Duluth, 55802

1-218-722-1273
1-800-423-1273
www.lsrm.org

The museum is located in Minnesota's Historic Union Depot. In 1969 the last train departed from the Depot and in 1973 work began to create the railroad museum. You will find that this is the location from which the North Shore Scenic Railroad train rides originate as well.

On display are steam, diesel and electric locomotives, passenger cars, freight cars, dining cars as well as equipment used in the logging and mining industries of Northern Minnesota. Look for the exhibits with hands-on activities that children will enjoy trying.

Included in the museum is Depot Square. This is a recreation of some of the businesses and shops found on the downtown Duluth streets in the 1910's. Through their storefronts, one can "window shop" back in time to view a meat and fish market, a barber shop and a drug store among many others.

Having grown up in Duluth in a railroad family, visits to the museum bring back many fond memories of our family train travels in the 50's and 60's. Marshall's Hardware, Duluth Tent & Awning and especially, Bridgeman's for ice cream, are stores included in the Square that were and still are favorites.

Admission to the museum is $12 for adults and $6 for children 3 to 13. Children 2 and under are free. The hours from Memorial Day to Labor Day are Monday through Saturday 9:30 AM to 6 PM and Sunday 9:30 AM to 5 PM. Then the hours open are 10 AM to 5 PM Monday through Saturday and 1 PM to 5 PM Sundays.

Note: Ask for a Tom's Top 10 Picks handout. His listing provides information on the locomotives and other railroad cars displayed.

*LAKE SUPERIOR ZOO
7210 Fremont St.
72nd Ave. W. & Grand Ave.
Duluth, 55807

1-218-730-4500 or 1-218-730-4900 (infoline)
www.lszoo.org

Upon entering the zoo, look for the Oh Fur Fun! Schedule of daily times for animal feedings and the planned, free event activities. Then plan to spend many hours exploring this easy to walk around and friendly staffed attraction.

In the Grigg's Learning Center, visitors are asked questions at displays like "What is a Reptile?" with answers provided. Here also are insects and small animals in glass houses. Look closely for the giant stick insect as large it is not.

In the Nocturnal Wing we watched the fruit bats being fed cut fruits and fruit juices. And we were told that if a bat is flying around us in the out of doors it is after the hovering mosquitoes. Go bats!

Trouble, an Alaskan brown grizzly bear, became our favorite. He came to the Duluth zoo from Alaska. The story now is that he broke into the Anchorage Zoo several times seeking the duck and goose food pellets. On one of his visits, this time to see Jake, the Anchorage Zoo's grizzly bear, he killed a goose; thus a trouble maker.

Open every day year around (except certain holidays) the summer hours are 10 AM to 5 PM and winter hours are 10 AM to 4 PM. Admission is $9 for ages 13 and older and $4 for children ages 3 to 12. Children 2 and younger are free. Group rates for 10 or more paid visitors are available with advance reservations (1-218-730-4500).

The zoo is 10 minutes from Duluth at the base of West Duluth's Spirit Mountain in Fairmont Park. Going north towards Duluth on Hwy. I-35 exit on Cody St. (251A) and follow the signs. Parking is free.

Note: Educational fun classes and events like Scout Programs, Boo at the Zoo and Zoo Camps are offered, too. For details on these and many others, visit the expanded website or call the education office at 1-218-730-4500 ext. 205.

*LOWER SIOUX AGENCY HISTORIC SITE
32469 Redwood Cty. Hwy. 2
Morton, 56270

1-507-697-6321
www.mnhs.org/places/sites/lsa

Located on Hwy. 2 nine miles East of Redwood Falls is a stone warehouse that today marks the site of the agency. This historic location was where the first organized Indian attack in the U.S.-Dakota Conflict of 1862 took place. A visitor's center tells the story of the Dakota Indians struggle against the white settlers whose building of farms reduced their hunting grounds and fur trading activities.

The hours are 10 AM to 5 PM Saturday and noon to 5 PM Sunday from Memorial Day through Labor Day. Group tours at other times can be arranged. Special events are held some summer weekends. Admission is from $4 to $6.

*MILLE LACS INDIAN MUSEUM
43411 Oodena Dr.
Onamia, 56359

1-320-532-3632
www.mnhs.org/places/sites/mlim

Located on Hwy. 169 on the southwest shore of Mille Lacs Lake 12 miles north of Onamia, this is the site of a museum and a trading post that have crafts and exhibits showing Ojibway culture.

Hours are Tuesday through Saturday 11 AM to 4 PM from Memorial Day through Labor Day. The restored 1939s trading post with its American Indian gifts from Mille Lacs artisans is then open in September, October and April, May on Wednesday through Saturday from 11 AM to 4 PM. Admission is from $5 to $7.

*NORTH SHORE SCENIC RAILROAD
The Depot
506 W. Michigan St.
Duluth, 55802

1-218-722-1273
1-800-423-1273
www.northshorescenicrailroad.org

As third generation members of a DM&IR railroad family, trains and train rides are very special to us; thus it is very nice to continue to be able to write about this activity. There are presently several different train ride choices. The Lester River ride is a one and one-half hour long round trip with 2 or 3 scheduled each day. The cost is $14 for adults and $7 for children ages 3 to 13.

The Two Harbors ride is a 6 hour round trip that includes a 2 hour layover in Two Harbors for exploring this pleasant town. This once a day scheduled trip begins at 10:30 AM Friday through Sunday. The cost is $28 for adults and $16 for children ages 3 through 13.

Pizza train rides are also regularly scheduled offerings. And special fall color trips are planned in September and October at the times the leaves are changing. Reservations are required for all but the Lester River rides.

Presently, the train rides are scheduled from mid-May through October. But because this is such a time-dependent adventure, confirming days and times is important to avoid disappointment.

Note: Birthday parties on the Birthday Caboose can be scheduled. The cost is $200 and includes the Lester River ride with pizza and cake. Call for the details.

*NORTH WEST COMPANY FUR POST
PO Box 51, 12551 Voyageur Lane
Pine City, 55063

1-320-629-6356
www.mnhs.org/places/sites/nwcfp

Located on Hwy. 7 only 1.5 miles West of Hwy. I-35 at exit 169, the site has recreated the 1804 post that for one winter was home for the traders of the British North West Company.

A short walk from the parking area takes one into the Visitor Center and its many exhibits and a gift shop. Exit the center to follow the appropriately named Snake River Trail along the Snake River to the outer post buildings. Along the walk stop to read the interesting messages on the signs.

One may be greeted at the stockades by men and women dressed in the clothing of this recreated era. These guides shares fascinating stories about life on the post. Much detail is given because of the journals which were kept by Mr. Sayers, the North West Company's representative at the post. At the reconstructed Wintering Post, a clerk explains the system of fur trade barter. It has many animal pelts hanging from the ceiling. These pelts are representative of the kinds traded and it was fun guessing the animals they came from. On the shelves were sponges, cloth, tools and beads. These were some of the items used to trade for the pelts. There is the possibility of observing the preparation of bannock, a griddlecake-like bread cooked over an open wood fire.

The post is open Monday and Thursday through Saturday from 10 AM to 5 PM and Sunday noon to 5 PM Memorial Day weekend through Labor Day. Other times can be arranged for groups through advance reservations. Admission is from $5 to $8.

*OLIVER H. KELLEY FARM
15788 Kelley Farm Rd.
Elk River, 55330

763-441-6896
www.mnhs.org/places/sites/ohkf

Located on Hwy. 10 only 2.5 miles Southeast of Elk River, this is the site of the founding of the Patrons of the Grange in 1867. It is now a living history farm that depicts farm life of the 1860s and 70s. Guides dressed in period clothing till the fields with oxen, horses and 19th century farm tools. The visitors center features an exhibit about Mr. Kelley and the Grange. Special events are held most weekends.

The farm and visitor center are open Wednesday through Saturday from 10 AM to 5 PM and Sunday from noon to 5 PM from Memorial Day weekend through Labor Day. In May and September, it is open weekend hours only. Admission is from $5 to $8.

*SPLIT ROCK LIGHTHOUSE HISTORIC SITE
3713 Split Rock Lighthouse Rd.
Two Harbors, 55616

1-218-226-6372
www.mnhs.org/places/sites/srl

Located in Split Rock Lighthouse State Park on Hwy. 61, 20 miles northeast of Two Harbors, the site includes the brick light tower, a fog-signal building, several lighthouse keepers' homes and the ruins of a tramway. The story of the lighthouse and development of the North Shore is shown on a video and in an exhibit at the visitors center. The lighthouse was built in 1910 and was in use for nearly 60 years. Special events are held on several weekends during the year.

Hours are 10 AM to 6 PM daily from mid-May through mid-October. Admission is from $5 to $8. From October to mid-May, days and hours are Thursday through Monday 11 AM to 4 PM when only the Visitor Center and Museum Store are open. There is no admission fee then but a state park vehicle permit is still required.

*S. S. WILLIAM A. IRVIN ORE BOAT MUSEUM
350 Harbor Dr.
Duluth Downtown Waterfront at Lake Ave.
Duluth, 55802

1-218-722-7876
www.williamairvin.com

For more than 40 years, the ship carried iron ore and coal on the Great Lakes and was once the flagship of the U.S. Steel's Great Lakes Fleet. It was retired because it was too small. However, during our tour led by a very informative guide, we found this hard to believe. We thought it hugh...especially the cargo holds.

The Irvin is longer than two football fields and the cargo area has enough space for 200 rail cars. For this tour, wear good walking shoes.

Tours of the Irvin are offered from April through October weather permitting. Check the website for scheduled start times. The 60 minute tour costs $10 for adults and $8 for students and seniors. Children 10 and under are free. Parking is $4 at the Duluth Entertainment Convention Center (DECC) (1-218-722-5573) located next to the Irvin.

TWEED MUSEUM OF ART
University of Minnesota Duluth
1201 Ordean Court
Duluth, 55812

1-218-726-8527
www.d.umn.edu/tma

Family Day at Tweed is a museum education event for all ages. Children must be accompanied by an adult as they participate together in the art activities and games. Actually Family Day is occasionally two days...a

Friday and Saturday or Saturday and Sunday. Drop in anytime between 2 PM and 4 PM for the fun. No reservations. Visit their website for the upcoming dates of the next Family Day(s). There is no fee but donations are welcome and appreciated.

Tweed also offers guided educational tours for grades K-12 Tuesday through Friday from 9 AM to 3 PM. The tour programs are planned as a student participation/interaction experience relating to a classroom subject of interest. The tour fee is $2 per student. There is no fee charged for the required chaperone needed for each 10 to 15 students. The maximum group size is 50. Contact the education director (1-218-726-8527) at least two weeks in advance for scheduling date desired.

Helpful websites, telephone numbers and addresses for planning visits to explore attractions outside the Twin Cities are listed here. And current road conditions and weather report information is available from the Minnesota Department of Transportation by calling 1-800-542-0220 or by visiting their website **www.511mn.org**

EXPLORE MINNESOTA TOURISM
121 7th Pl. E., Suite 100, St. Paul, 55101
651-296-5029 or 1-800-657-3700
www.exploreminnesota.com
Friendly contacts for planning regional travel including information on parks, campgrounds, boat rentals, resorts and festivals.

AUSTIN CONVENTION & VISITORS BUREAU/CVB
104 11th Ave. NW, Suite D, Austin, 55912
1-800-444-5713 or 1-507-437-4563
www.austincvb.com
Attraction: SPAM Museum

BRAINERD LAKES CHAMBER
124 N. 6th St., Brainerd, 56401
1-800-450-2838 or 1-218-829-2838
www.explorebrainerdlakes.com
Attractions: Paul Bunyan Nature Learning Center, Paul Bunyan Trail, Paul Bunyan Land at This Old Farm Pioneer Village

CHISHOLM AREA CHAMBER OF COMMERCE
223 W. Lake St., Chisholm, 55719
1-800-422-0806 or 1-218-254-7930
www.chisholmchamber.com
Attractions: Minnesota Discovery Center, Minnesota Museum of Mining

VISIT DULUTH

21 W. Superior St. Suite 100, Duluth, 55802
1-800-4DULUTH
www.visitduluth.com
Attractions: Aerial Lift Bridge, Canal Park, The Depot, Lake Superior
Zoo, Lakewalk, Park Point, Playfront, Spirit Mountain

ELY CHAMBER OF COMMERCE

1600 E. Sheridan St., Ely, 55731
1-800-777-7281 or 1-218-365-6123
www.ely.org
Attractions: BWCA, International Wolf Center, North American Bear
Center

FARGO/MOORHEAD CONVENTION & VISITORS BUREAU

2001 44th St. SW, Fargo, ND 58103
1-800-235-7654 or 1-701-282-3653
www.fargomoorhead.org
Attractions: Children's Museum at Yunker Farm, Comstock House,
Scandinavian Hjemkomst Festival

GRAND MARAIS VISITOR CENTER

PO Box 1048, 13 N. Broadway, Grand Marais, 55604
1-888-922-5000
www.grandmarais.com
Attractions: Boundary Waters Canoe Area (BWCA), Grand Portage
National Monument & Heritage Center, Gunflint Trail

GRAND RAPIDS TOURISM

501 S. Pokegama Ave., Suite 3, Grand Rapids, 55744
1-800-355-9740 or 1-218-326-9607
www.visitgrandrapids.com
Attractions: Forest History Center, Judy Garland Museum & Birthplace

INTERNATIONAL FALLS AREA CHAMBER OF COMMERCE/CVB

301 2nd Ave., International Falls, 56649
1-800-325-5766
www.rainylake.org
Attractions: Gold Mine, Ice Box Days, Smokey Bear Park, Voyageurs
National Park

LAKE CITY AREA CHAMBER OF COMMERCE

101 W. Center St., Lake City, 55041
1-800-369-4123 or 1-651-345-4123
www.lakecity.org
Attractions: Frontenac State Park, Hok-Si-La Park, Pearl of the Lake Paddleboat

LITTLE FALLS CONVENTION & VISITORS BUREAU

606 SE 1st St., Little Falls, 56345
1-800-325-5916 or 1-320-616-4959
www.littlefallsmn.com
Attractions: Camp Ripley Environmental Center, Charles A. Lindbergh Site and State Park, Charles A. Weyerhaeuser Museum, Minnesota Fishing Museum and Education Center

GREATER MANKATO CONVENTION & VISITOR BUREAU

1 Civic Center Plaza, Suite 200, Mankato 56002
1-800-657-4733 or 1-507-385-6660
www.greatermankato.com
Attractions: Betsy-Tacy Self-Guided Walking Tour, Viking Football Training Camp

MILLE LACS AREA TOURISM COUNCIL

PO Box 286, Isle, 56342
1-888-350-2692
www.millelacs.com
Attractions: Father Hennepin State Park, Mille Lacs Indian Museum & Trading Post

NEW ULM CHAMBER OF COMMERCE/CVB

PO Box 384, 1 N. Minnesota, New Ulm, 56073
1-888-463-9856 or 1-507-233-4300
www.newulm.com
Attractions: Bavarian Blast, Town Square Glockenspiel

PIPESTONE CHAMBER & VISITOR'S BUREAU

PO Box 8, 117 8th Ave. S. E., Pipestone, 56164
1-800-336-6125
www.pipestoneminnesota.com
Attractions: Fort Pipestone, Peace Pipe at Rock Island Depot, Pipestone County Museum, Pipestone National Monument

REDWOOD FALLS AREA CHAMBER & TOURISM

200 S. Mill St., Redwood Falls, 56283
1-800-657-7070 or 1-507-637-2828
www.redwoodfalls.org
Attractions: Laura Ingalls Wilder Museum & Pageant, Lower Sioux
Agency History Site, Sod House on the Prairie

TWO HARBORS AREA CHAMBER OF COMMERCE/
INFORMATION CENTER

1330 Hwy. 61, Two Harbors, 55616
1-800-777-7384
www.twoharborschamber.com
Attractions: Edna G Tugboat, John Bear Grease Dog Race, Ore Docks,
Split Rock Lighthouse, Winter Frolic

WINDOM AREA CHAMBER OF COMMERCE/CVB

303 9th St., Windom, 56101
1-800-794-6366 or 1-507-831-2752
www.winwacc.com
Attractions: Jeffers Petroglyphs, Riverfest

NOTES

SEASONAL EVENTS

SEASONAL EVENTS

For up-to-date information on the event, check the local newspapers, websites and/or call during the season.

SPRING

CINCO DE MAYO FIESTA – May
Riverview Economic Development Association (REDA)
176 Cesar Chavez
St. Paul, 55107

651-222-6347
www.districtdelsol.com

Cinco de Mayo, May 5th is an important Mexican national holiday. It celebrates the Mexican victory over the French colonial troops in Puebla, Mexico on May 5, 1862. On St. Paul's West Side, Cinco de Mayo is celebrated over the closest weekend in May with an outdoor festival on Cesar Chavez. Mexican bands, folk dancers and children's groups perform on 4 stages spread from Wabasha to Anita. Other activities include a fiesta parade on Saturday morning at 10, live Latin music, food and a children's area with face painting, storytelling and other cultural activities. This is a lively, colorful celebration of Hispanic culture and tradition.

*CIRCUSES – April

Everybody loves a circus! In the Twin Cities we are visited twice yearly by two different circuses. The St. Paul Osman Temple Shrine Circus (651-452-5662) **www.osmancircus.com** performs in State Fair Coliseum in March or early April. In October, the Minneapolis Zuhrah Shrine Club Circus (612-871-3555) performs at the Target Center (612-673-1313) **www.targetcenter.com** and click on Event Calendar. Ticket prices vary from $10 to $25 with some local stores offering discount coupons. Contact the respective website or ticket office for information on admission fees, current locations and dates.

EARTH DAY – April

Founded in 1970 by Gaylord Nelson, former Wisconsin governor and U.S. senator, to educate people about the importance of protecting the environment. The officially designated Earth Day is April 22. However, events are held throughout the week leading up to E-Day. Activity announcements appear in the newspapers and as features on local TV newscasts. The website **www.earthday.org** also locates and provides details on scheduled programs and events in your area by searching on city or zipcode. Most are free with some having a small admission or ticket fee.

*FESTIVAL OF NATIONS – April & May
International Institute of Minnesota
1694 Como Ave.
St. Paul, 55108

651-647-0191 ext. 300
www.festivalofnations.com

This unique festival is an annual event held for four days Thursday through Sunday in late April into early May. It fills the St. Paul Rivercentre on Kellogg Blvd. in St. Paul with as many as 90 ethnic groups coming from throughout Minnesota. People dressed in the costumes of their heritage set up booths of crafts for sale in the bazaar, have displays of their customs and culture in the exhibit area and sell foods of their heritage in the ethnic cafes. Programs of dance, song and music are continuous throughout the festival as are the many folk art demonstrations. It is best to locate a program immediately upon entering, select those events not to be missed and then just wander to discover. Admission is $12.50 for adults and $7 for children 5 to 16. Children under 5 are free when accompanied by an adult. Advance discount tickets are available.

Note: School Groups Student Days for grades 6 and up are Thursday and Friday. Special hours are set aside for these visits. Advance school group tickets are sold through the Festival of Nations office only. Call 651-647-0101 ext. 309.

*FLINT HILLS INTERNATIONAL CHILDREN'S FESTIVAL – May & June
Ordway Center for the Performing Arts
345 Washington St.
St. Paul, MN 55102

651-224-4222
www.ordway.org

First held in 2001, this 6-day festival for school groups and children accompanied by adults is held within the Ordway and in surrounding parks in downtown St. Paul late May into early June. Primarily for ages 5 to 14, the festival is one of Ordway's efforts to provide more arts experiences for children. All activities, which adults will enjoy as well, include theater, music and dance, have international ties. Festival Family

Days are on Saturday and Sunday and the 4 Festival School Days are on weekdays. Family Days ticketed performances are $5 each. The School Days performances are subsidized by the Ordway. The outdoor festival activities are free. Food for purchase is available. Click on Tickets/Events on website for current details.

LLAMA MAGIC/SHEPHERD'S HARVEST SHEEP & WOOL FESTIVAL – May
Washington County Fairgrounds
Cty. Rd. 15 & State Hwy. 5
12300 N. 40 St.
Lake Elmo, 55042
1-715-246-5837
www.llamamagic.com
www.shepherdsharvestfestival.org

This very special and unique event is really two. Held on Mother's Day weekend in May, the Shepherd's Harvest is a Sheep and Wool Festival with many planned children's activities including hands-on working with wool to make something, perhaps a bracelet, to take home. Each year a class for children is offered, too. One year it was felting on a bar of soap. Live animal demonstrations include sheepshearing and herding dogs.

Llama Magic is also family-oriented. At the show clinic, children as young as 7 can learn how to handle a llama in the show ring. Children can take a llama for a walk around the fairgrounds. The llama and alpaca show is for spectators with the Llama Limbo, if scheduled, a must see. Children's craft activities might include making a felt ball necklace from llama fiber.

A delicious lamb burger or bratwurst lunch is available at a very modest cost. Try one before sold out as they go quickly. A variety of other kinds of foods are available for purchase, too. Or bring your own picnic lunch and snacks to eat at one of the many picnic tables on the grounds. Gates are open from 9 AM to 5 PM Saturday and 10 AM to 5 PM Sunday. Parking is free.

MAYDAY PARADE & FESTIVAL – May
In the Heart of the Beast Puppet and Mask Theatre (HOBT)
1500 E. Lake St.
Minneapolis, 55407

612-721-2535
www.hobt.org

Each year a new theme is selected for this parade which features fantastic, giant puppets and masks. One year the theme was Leap into the

Wonderous Possible. During the month of April, many of the masks and puppets are made in volunteer Tuesday and Thursday evening and Saturday workshops open to children and adults.

The parade is always held on the first Sunday of May beginning at 1 PM on Bloomington Ave. S. and 25th St. It joyously travels to Powderhorn Park at 34th St and 15th Ave. S. where the festivities continue with puppet performances, music, food and the Tree of Life Ceremony. Call the theatre or visit its website for up-to-date details.

MEMORIAL DAY EVENTS – May
Lakewood Cemetery
3600 Hennepin Ave.
Hennepin Ave. S. & 36th St.
Minneapolis, 55408

612-822-2171
www.lakewoodcemetery.com

From morning to late afternoon, many activities are planned for families. Beginning with a traditional Memorial Day ceremony, visitors can go on to learn about cemetery lore. It could be cemetery symbols and art or family history. Each year the theme changes but is always educational. Did you know that a tulip is a declaration of love or sunflowers mean adoration? Gravestone-rubbings is one activity children can try. Trolley ride tours are offered. Live music can be enjoyed, too. Click on Tours & Events on the website for all the details.

*MINNESOTA HORSE EXPO – April
State Fairgrounds
1265 Snelling Ave. N.
St. Paul, 55108

952-922-8666
1-877-462-8758
www.mnhorseexpo.org

Sponsored by the Minnesota Horse Council, this discovered, close to home event, is held most often over the last weekend in April on the Minnesota State Fairgrounds. Over 300 horses are on display in the Horse Barn. Clydesdales, Norwegian Fjords, Aztec and Miniatures are just a few of the breeds visitors can see and talk about with their owners and trainers. The Children's Area is in the Sheep Barn.

Everyone is invited to enjoy the free horse wagon rides. A daily Parade of Breeds is held between noon and 1 in the Coliseum Arena. And there are over 600 booths to browse among for horse information, products and services. Pick up a free schedule of events upon arrival. Admission is $9 for adults and $6 for seniors and children ages 6 to 12. Parking on the Fair grounds is free.

Note: At **www.horsetraildirectory.com** a directory of Minnesota horse trails can be found by selecting the option "riding trails" and specifying state Minnesota. More information can be found at the DNR website **www.dnr.state.mn.us/horseback_riding,** including how to purchase the horse pass required for trailriding on all DNR-administered Minnesota land.

SYTTENDE MAI (NORWEGIAN CONSTITUTION DAY) – May
Sons of Norway
1455 W. Lake St.
Minneapolis, 55408

612-827-3611
1-800-945-8851
www.sofn.com
www.mindekirken.org

Local Norwegians like to celebrate two days a year which have special meaning to them and friends of Norway. Syttende Mai is May 17th, Norway's Constitution Day. It is celebrated the weekend closest to the 17th.

On Saturday in Loring Park at Yale Place and Willow in Minneapolis, the program and entertainment begin at noon with singing of the national anthem. Activities including demonstrations and performances follow. There is a parade, games for children, wood carving, singing, dancing and more.

On Sunday the festivities begin with the Syttende Mai Festival Service at 11 AM in the Norwegian Lutheran Memorial Church, 924 E. 21st St. in Minneapolis. This is followed by a meandering noon parade through the neighborhood ending at the church for refreshments, games for children and folk dancing. Contact the Sons of Norway or visit the websites for all the current details. Norway Day, the other special day, is celebrated in June and is included in the summer seasonal events.

Kom og kos deg med oss!
(Come and enjoy yourself with us!)

SUMMER

AQUATENNIAL – July
Minneapolis Downtown Council
81 S. 9th St. Suite 260
Minneapolis, 55402

612-338-3807
www.aquatennial.com

Beginning the third week in July, Minneapolis hosts their Ten Best Days of Summer festival honoring Minneapolis lakes and rivers. Many traditional family and youth events and activities are held during this celebration including the mid-week evening Torchlight Parade. Lake Calhoun is the location for the Milk Carton Boat Races, Sand Sculpturing and Sand Castle competition and sailing regatta. The end of the festival is concluded with a spectacular fireworks show launched over the Mississippi River. This is a celebration not to be missed. During the Aquatennial, the local newspapers list the daily events with their times and locations. A visit to the website provides events information as well.

CANADIAN DAYS – August
Little Canada City Center
515 Little Canada Rd. E.
Little Canada, 55117

651-766-4029
www.ci.little-canada.mn.us

Held over the first full weekend in August, this three day weekend celebration is at Spooner Park, Little Canada. Friday night is Corn Feed night. With the purchase of the child-designed Canadian Day button for $2, you receive free entrance to the Corn Feed. Saturday the kiddie parade begins at 10 AM and features kiddie floats, wagons and children in costume. The parade starts at Little Canada Elementary School and goes one block to the park.

L. C.'s Playland returns each year. This is a penny carnival style playland with games and prizes. Other family events include carnival rides for all ages, a pancake breakfast, a Saturday night fireworks show and evening music for street dancing for all ages. The grand finale is the Grand Parade on Sunday at 1 PM.

DANISH DAY – June
Danish American Fellowship/Danebo
3030 W. River Pkwy. S.
Minneapolis, 55406

612-729-3800
www.danebo.org

All Danes look forward to this festival held the Sunday in June closest to Denmark's Constitution Day, June 5th. Held on the grounds of Danebo, folk dancing, Danish music, games and Danish craft and information booths are all a part of the celebration that begins with Danish pastries at 10:30 AM. Children of all ages can compete in Viking swordplay held in the Viking tent that has many Viking items on display, too. Open-faced sandwiches and other delicious Danish foods are available for sale. If the weather is uncooperative, some of the festival activities move into the building.

DEUTSCHER TAGE (GERMAN DAY) – June
Germanic-American Institute
301 Summit Ave.
St. Paul, 55102

651-222-7027 (infoline)
www.gai-mn.org

On the second weekend in June, Deutscher Tage is held at the Kulturhaus grounds on Summit Ave. from 11 AM to 6 PM. Schuhplattlers and Edelweiss dancers perform their special dances. German foods can be purchased to eat. There are singalongs, bands and more dancing. Booths are set-up displaying travel information about Germany and selling items having to do with Germany and German heritage. It's a fun time especially when a singalong gets started.

Note: The Kulturhaus House office is open from 10 AM to 4:30 PM on Monday through Friday. Special events and dinners are held monthly throughout the year. Contact the Germanic-American Institute for information on these events, too.

GRAND OLD DAY – June
Grand Ave. Business Association
649 Grand Ave.
St. Paul, 55105

651-699-0029
www.grandave.com

Majestic Grand Avenue, in the Summit Hill/MacCalester Groveland area of St. Paul, is fun for families to explore during this celebration held on the first Sunday in June. The day's festivities start off with competitive inline skate and running races at 7:30 AM. A half mile youth run and walk/jog events are at 8:45 AM. The Children's Parade is at 10 AM with registration for it at 9:30. The Grand Old Day Parade begins at 10:15 AM at Fairview and Grand and continues for several miles east along Grand to Dale. A Family Fun area is set-up on the grounds of Ramsey Jr. High at Grand and Cambridge. Entertainment continues all day for children and parents. Clowns, bands and other activities are planned to make the day fun for families. The day's activities end at 5 PM.

HIGHLAND FEST – July
Highland Business Association
790 Cleveland Ave. S. Suite 219
St. Paul, 55116

651-699-9042 (infoline)
www.highlandfest.com

During the third full weekend in July, this festival is held in the Highland Village neighborhood of St. Paul. Most activities take place around Ford Parkway and S. Cleveland Ave. Most children's activities are on Saturday between 10 AM and 2 PM. In past years they have included pony rides, a petting zoo and face painting.

HIGHLAND PARK WATER TOWER – July
SE Corner of Snelling Ave. S. & Ford Pkwy.
St. Paul, 55116

651-266-6350
www.stpaul.gov/index.aspx

For spectacular views of the Twin Cities, climb the 151 steps of this 127 foot tall historic and still operating water tower in July during Highland Fest. With a chair or bench on each of the many landings, even the smallest child can make the climb. The open-air observation deck has benches, too, for resting or for the young to stand on. The views from the top include the International Airport over 3 miles away, downtown Minneapolis 6 miles away and downtown St. Paul 4 miles. Very knowledgeable St. Paul Water Utility employees are present from 9 AM to 5 PM during the Open House event held during Highland Park's Highland Fest celebration. Postcards are for sale. Pamphlets on water quality and an "I saw St. Paul from the Top of the Highland Tower" sticker are free and can be picked up on the ground level.

IRISH FAIR OF MINNESOTA – August
Harriet Island in St. Paul
836 Prior Ave. N.
St. Paul, 55104

952-474-7411 (infoline)
www.irishfair.com

Held on the second full weekend in August, the fair has become one of the biggest celebrations of Irish culture in the Midwest. The Children's Area on the grounds provide lots of entertainment and activities for "the wee ones." Under a large tent covering many tables, clothespin doll dressing, picture painting and clay animals maybe crafted. Games, shows, sheepdog demonstrations, music, dance and storytelling events are scheduled each day. Irish Soda bread is for sale.

The fair opens Friday with entertainment events at 3 PM, at 10 AM on Saturday and at 9 AM on Sunday for a church service followed by activities at 10 AM.

NORWAY DAY – July
Norwegian National League of Minnesota

612-861-4793
www.sofn-1.com
www.sofn.com

This special day for Norwegians and friends is held on the second Sunday in July in Minnehaha Park. The event starts at 10 AM with a church service and continues with a Children's Flag Parade, Norwegian folk dancing, bands playing Norwegian music and booths set up typical of a small Norwegian fair. The Viking Age Club performs, also. Refreshments featuring Scandinavian cookies and open-faced sandwiches are available. Check the websites for current details.

Gratulerer med dagen!
(Congratulations with the day.)

PAWS ON GRAND – August
Grand Ave. Business Association
649 Grand Ave.
St. Paul, 55105

651-699-0029
www.grandave.com

For dog owners, this event on the first Sunday in August is described as a time to "pause" to walk your dog with family and friends on the Avenue.

Pets will be provided treats, toys, pet tags, pet food, photo ops and more. A great time to see lots of different breeds of dogs. Children will find this event lots of fun.

POLISH FESTIVAL – August
2514 Central Ave. NE
Minneapolis, MN 55418

612-387-9291
www.tcpolishfestival.org

Held on Old Main St. across from Riverplace and St. Anthony Main the second weekend in August, this is a newly discovered festival in our Twin Cities area. It's event highlights include a children's area, a Polish sheep dog exhibition, storytellers, singalongs and free polka lessons.

RONDO DAYS FESTIVAL – July
Rondo Ave. Inc.
1360 University Ave. #140
St. Paul, 55104

651-459-1078
www.rondodays.com

Held on the third Saturday in July, this is a reunion of sorts. The celebration activities are a way of carrying on the traditions of the former Rondo neighborhood, once the center of St. Paul's black community, that in the 1960's was eliminated with the construction of Hwy. 94. The former Rondo Road is now Concordia Ave. in St. Paul. Today, the day is filled with music of all types from the blues to hip-hop. Drill teams from many states compete at St. Paul Central's stadium. Other activities include the Rondo Days Grand Parade, musical performances on the Rondo Entertainment Stage and many booths providing information on the community. Spicy ribs and corn on the cob are just a few of the tasty food items for sale. The festival is for people of all races, ages and communities. The Martin Luther King Park, 271 Mackubin St., St. Paul, is the central location for the activities. Call Rondo Ave. Inc. or visit the website for the current year's program. And don't miss the fun!

ST. ANTHONY PARK ARTS FESTIVAL – June
Carter & Como Aves.
St. Paul, 55108

651-642-0411
www.stanthonyparkartsfestival.org

Traditionally held the first Saturday in June, this annual neighborhood event happens on Como from Carter to Luther Place in St. Anthony Park. The festival emphasizes books, crafts, food and family entertainment. Children will have fun picking out books at the library's used book sale, eating ice cream treats, listening to musical entertainment and watching a magic show or street corner juggler. A Children's Art Activity Tent is set-up at Luther Place. Adults will enjoy the many craft stalls on the lawns of the library and Luther Seminary and browsing through the bookbins of Micawber's. Look for Speedy Market's food wagon for their special brats, hot dogs, burgers and drinks. Good eats at reasonable prices. The festival is from 9:30 AM to 5:30 PM.

SVENSKARNAS DAG /SWEDISH HERITAGE DAY – June
www.SvenskarnasDag.com

The Swedish residents (and non-Swedish who want to attend) gather each year on the 4th Sunday in June in Minnehaha Park to celebrate with a morning church service, raising of the Midsommar Pole, dancing, music and enjoying Swedish foods. The highlight of the day is the crowning of the Midsummer Queen during the afternoon program. For more information on the day's activities, visit the website.

TWIN CITIES AMERICAN INDIAN ARTS FESTIVAL – June
Native American Community Development Institute (NACDI)
1414 E. Franklin Ave.
Minneapolis, 55404

612-235-4976
www.allmyrelationsarts.com/fesitval

This annual outdoor festival includes exhibits and demonstrations of American Indian arts and cultural dances and music. Held on the 2nd weekend in June from noon to 8 PM each day, the event takes place on the Green Space next to the Minneapolis American Indian Center located at 16th Ave. S and Franklin Ave. in South Minneapolis.

See pow-wow dances, listen to singers featuring jing traditional songs, taste Indian tacos and observe demonstrations that could include porcupine quilling. One can't miss the many teepees on the grounds. Ask the people nearby for help in interpretation of the symbols decorating the exteriors. Children can participate in activities that could include making a dream catcher or Ojibwe Bandolier bag. These are just a few of the many attractions all who attend can enjoy at this family friendly festival.

NOTES

FALL

ANOKA HALLOWEEN PARADES – October
12 Bridge Square
Anoka, 55303

763-421-7130
www.anokahalloween.com

Anoka, Halloween capitol of the world, holds a big week-long event with 3 parades to celebrate this time of the year. The Light Up the Night parade is the first and is held on the next to last Saturday at 7 PM on Main Street. The Big Parade of Little People is at 1:15 PM on the following Friday and includes elementary school children in costume and the junior high school marching bands. The next day, the Grand Day parade, a gigantic extravaganza of marching bands, clowns, queens, animals and all sorts of marvelous floats parades down Main St. beginning at 1 PM and lasting 2 hours. Other activities held during the week long festivities include a 5K foot race for all family members and the Ambassador Coronation. Another continuing tradition is the Big Haunted House sponsored by the Knights of Columbus and held at the Anoka County Fairgrounds. Look for Key Dates on their website for all the event details.

BOO BASH ON GRAND AVENUE – October
Grand Ave. Business Association
649 Grand Ave.
St. Paul, 55105

651-699-0029
www.grandave.com

The Boo Bash is an event on Grand Ave. for families who like to celebrate Halloween together by dressing up in costume and meandering the Avenue gathering treats. The little ones with the Moms, the Dads and even some family pets in costume enjoy the activities held on the Avenue the Sunday before Halloween. Besides the goodies given out by local businesses to children 12 and under, there are pony rides, a petting zoo and a children's costume contest. This event is fun to see as well as participate in.

CARNIVAL OF THE ARTS – October
Edina Art Center
4701 W. 64th St.
Edina, 55435

952-903-5780
www.EdinaArtCenter.com

This is a Free Family Fun Day event held on a Sunday afternoon early in October. Hands-on children's art activities, artist demonstrations, refreshments and performances by local talent make this a most enjoyable event for all ages. Visit their website or call for the current date and details.

*CIRCUSES – October

Everybody loves a circus! In the Twin Cities we are visited twice yearly by two different circuses. The St. Paul Osman Temple Shrine Circus (651-452-5662) **www.osmancircus.com** performs at the State Fair Coliseum in March or early April. In October, the Minneapolis Zuhrah Shrine Club Circus (612-871-3555) **www.zuhrah.org** performs at the Target Center (612-673-1313) **www.targetcenter.com** and click on Events. Ticket prices vary from $10 to $25 with some local stores offering discount coupons. Contact the respective website or ticket office for information on admission fees, current locations and dates.

CZECH SLOVAK FESTIVAL – September
CSPS Hall
West 7 St. & Western Ave.
383 Michigan St.
St. Paul, 55102

651-290-0542 (infoline)
www.sokolmn.org

The second Saturday in September is for celebrating Czechoslovakian heritage. The event, held at the Highland Park Pavilion, 1200 Montreal Ave. in St. Paul, begins with a noon flag ceremony and continues until 5 PM with music, food, games, dancing and singing. Food includes ethnic goodies like Czech Booya and sausages as well as American favorites. There are craft booths and displays, too. For more the information about this special day, another contact number is 612-920-5949.

HIGHLAND PARK WATER TOWER – October
SE Corner of Snelling Ave. S. & Ford Pkwy.
St. Paul, 55116

651-266-6350
www.stpaul.gov/index.aspx

Climb the 151 steps of this 127 foot tall historic and still operating water tower the second weekend in October for the beautiful fall foliage views. With a chair or bench on each landing every 15 to 20 steps, even the smallest child can make the climb. The observation deck has benches, too, for resting or for the young to stand on. The views from the top include the International Airport over 3 miles away, downtown Minneapolis 6 miles away and downtown St. Paul 4 miles. Very knowledgeable St. Paul Water Utility employees are on duty from 9 AM to 5 PM during the tower's Fall Open House. Postcards are for sale. Pamphlets on water quality are free. And an "I saw St. Paul from the Top of the Highland Tower" sticker is your reward when returning to ground level.

*RENAISSANCE FESTIVAL – August & September
Mid-America Festivals
Corporate Office Suite 306
1244 S. Canterbury Rd.
Shakopee, 55379

952-445-7361
1-800-966-8215 (infoline)
www.renaissancefest.com

The festival offers many fascinating things for everyone of all ages. It is the recreation of a 16th century celebration complete with authentically costumed musicians, dancers, mimes, cooks, beggars and other characters of the time. There are craftsmen in thatched huts selling their wares and demonstrating how they are made. Games of skill like archery and fencing, King's Joust and the Queens Darts can be tried. Daily special events include authentic real armored jousting, strolling minstrels, puppeteers and magicians. Everywhere there is food to purchase like Scotch eggs, corn on the cob, roasted sausages and cheeses and breads. Located 7 miles south of Shakopee on Highway 169, the festival is open 9 AM to 7 PM weekends and Labor Day from mid-August through late September. Parking and all entertainment are included in the admission fee that is $20.95 for adults, $18.95 for seniors, $11.95 for children ages 5 to 12 and free for children under 5.

*SEVER'S CORN MAZE & FALL FESTIVAL – September & October
Shakopee, 55379

952-974-5000 (infoline)
www.severscornmaze.com

The Corn Maze, America's largest, has been recreated each year since 1997 by the Peterson family. Each year they build a different one. One year, in partnership with the Minnesota Vikings' celebration of its 50th season, the maze incorporated a symbol of the helmeted Viking complete with horns.

On the website is information on the history of the maze, a graphic of this year's maze and directions with map to the maze. Shows and attractions, fun and games and a brief weather report are here, too.

The site is open weekends from mid-September through October from 11 AM to 6 PM. Admission is $11 for ages 4 and older. Ages 3 and under are free. A discount coupon is available on the website. The location is in Shakopee off Highway169 S. and Canterbury Rd. next to Canterbury Park. Look for their signs.

*STATE FAIR – August & September
Midway Pkwy. & Snelling Ave.
1265 Snelling Ave. N.
St. Paul, 55108

651-288-4400
www.mnstatefair.org

This is one of the largest fairs in the nation. Held for 12 days, it starts the last week of August and always ends on Labor Day. On designated Kids Days, children 5 to 12 are admitted for $7. Children will find many things of interest at the fair including the cattle barns, horse barns, machinery hill, and the activities and displays in the education, natural resources and 4-H buildings. Children have their own animal barnyard at the Children's FFA Barnyard. Not to be missed is the Children's Theater Stage where the attractions are planned for families. The show might include a juggler, science show, flea circus or magician. The shows last about 30 minutes, are free and are repeated throughout each day.

Take a least one ride down the Giant Slide. Have a least one corn dog. And share a bag of mini donuts.

Gate admissions to the fair are $12 for adults, $10 for children 5 to 12 and $10 for seniors 65 and older. Children under 5 are free. Tickets purchased in advance are discounted. The gates open at 6 AM and close at 10 PM. Most exhibit building hours are 9 to 9 daily. Parking on the fairgrounds is $12.

NOTES

BLACK HISTORY CELEBRATIONS

The months of January and February offer opportunities to learn about black leaders and black history through many community events and activities.

MLK Day of Service, a tribute to Martin Luther King Jr., is a morning of action and community service. This event begins with breakfast at the Minneapolis Community & Technical College (MC&TC) **www.minneapolis.edu**, 1501 Hennepin Ave., Minneapolis, on or close to Dr. King's January 15 birthdate. Attendees listen to an inspirational speaker and then go out into the community for a morning of volunteer service. All ages are welcome. Family participation is encouraged, too. For additional information visit the website or call 612-659-6315.

The Science Museum of Minnesota **www.ssm.org** holds **African Americans in Science Day** on a Saturday in February. The event provides children the opportunity to do science projects with local scientists and engineers. The activities are free with the admission fee to the museum. No reservations. Recorded information 651-221-9444.

The General Mills Foundation and UNCF support and sponsor the Annual Dr. Martin Luther King, Jr. Holiday Breakfast each year on or close to his birthdate. The neighborhood community breakfasts, which require reservations, begin at 7 AM. At 8 AM the event's keynote speaker's address is broadcast live from the Minneapolis Convention Center to all other locations. Visit **www.mlkbreakfast.org** to register to attend a **MLK Breakfast** in your local community and for other details.

*A CHRISTMAS CAROL – November & December
Guthrie Theater
818 2nd St. S.
Minneapolis, 55415

612-377-2224
1-877- 44STAGE
www.guthrietheater.org

During its 35-year run, this theatrical adaptation of Charles Dickens' *A Christmas Carol* has become a holiday tradition. Older children will understand and enjoy the play that is performed from mid-November through December. The costumes, stage setting and special effects as well as the acting are always outstanding. When Marley's ghost ascends from below stage in a cloud of misty smoke, everyone in the audience shudders as he moans and his chains clink. Scrooge is wonderfully transformed from a greedy miser to a generous uncle during the production. This is a very popular seasonal treat with tickets becoming available for purchase as early as September. Call or visit the website for performance dates and times. Ticket prices range from $30 to $70.

*FAMILY CONCERTS – February & March & April
Music in the Park Series
The Schubert Club
75 5th St. W. Suite 302
St. Paul, 55102

651-645-5699
www.schubertorg/musicinthepark/family

Three different concerts are held each winter series. Children along with their family members will enjoy listening to and participating in the folk, ethnic and classical performances of the children friendly artists.

In a large room with children seated on the floor up close to the performers and adults seated in back on folding chairs or standing holding the younger ones, the concert begins with introductions. Then there are the reminders to listen with your ears and look with your eyes and move to the sounds.

As the concert continues, children maybe invited to come forward and participate in making music. This produces lots of smiles.

Concerts are Friday evenings at 6:15 and repeated at 7:30 at St. Matthew's Episcopal Church in St. Anthony Park, 2136 Carter Ave., St. Paul, 55108. A 3-concert season ticket is $15. Single tickets are $6. As the concerts are very popular and often sold out, it is best to purchase early to avoid disappointments.

*FILM SOCIETY OF MINNEAPOLIS/ST. PAUL – December
St. Anthony Main Theatre
115 SE Main St.
Minneapolis, 55414

612-331-7563 or 612-331-3134 (infoline)
www.mspfilmsociety.org

In the week following Christmas, the Film Society (formerly Minnesota Film Arts) traditionally shows the film, *Ronya, the Robber's Daughter,* based on the Astrid Lindgren novel. To receive more information, visit their website or contact them directly. Admission is $6 for adults and $6 for children.

GERMAN CHRISTMAS CELEBRATION – November or December
Germanic-American Institute (GAI)
301 Summit Ave.
St. Paul, 55102

651-222-7027 (infoline)
www.gai-mn.org

On a Sunday afternoon in late November or early December, the German Kulturhaus on Summit Ave. holds Open Haus from 11 AM to 4 PM. The Volksfest Singers give a concert of German Christmas carols. And visitors are invited to join in the singing. Other activities include tours of the house beautifully decked out with wreaths, tinsel and Christmas trees featuring traditional decorations like candy canes and candles.

GRAND MEANDER – December
Grand Ave. Business Association
649 Grand Ave.
St. Paul, 55105

651-699-0029
www.grandave.com

On the first Saturday in December from 8:30 AM to the early evening hours, the Grand Ave. merchants invite families to spend the day exploring the avenue. There one can find a breakfast with Santa, Christmas carolers, free soup tasting, holiday characters, Santa's reindeer, roasted chestnuts and free horse-drawn hayrides. Also catch a free ride on the Grand Avenue Express, a Victorian-style trolley powered by natural gas. Sounds like fun. It is. Bundle up and enjoy the day.

HOLIDAZZLE PARADES – November & December
Minneapolis Downtown Council
81 S. 9th St. Suite 260
Minneapolis, 55402

612-338-3807
www.holidazzle.com

This holiday tradition is held on Nicollet Mall from late November through mid-December, Thursday through Sunday evenings beginning at 6:30 PM. The parade winds down Nicollet Mall for 30 minutes. Each parade is different. Lighted floats, musical groups and other surprises entertain the parade watchers. One might see a lighted 60-foot Chinese dragon or Santabear in a sleigh. A very family-oriented event featuring nursery rhyme and storybook costumed entertainers, this is a delightful parade we hope continues for a long time. And of course Santa Claus always makes an appearance. One of the sponsors of the parades is the Minneapolis Downtown Council. For more information, contact them at 612-376-SNOW or visit the website.

*JAPANESE NEW YEAR CELEBRATION – January

The Japan America Society of Minnesota (JASM) celebrates the new year with this family festival to which everyone is invited. The party is generally held from 4 to 8 PM on a Sunday in mid-January with the location varying from year to year. There is typically Japanese drumming performances, artists demonstrating Japanese cartoon drawing called manga and special games for children as well as traditional music and dance. Admission is $20 to $25 for a family package, $10 to $15 for adults, seniors and students. Children under 5 are free. For current date and details, contact JASM at 612-627-9357 or visit their website at **www.mn-japan.org**.

*KWANZAA FAMILY CELEBRATION – December
Minnesota History Center (MHC)
345 Kellogg Blvd. W.
St. Paul, 55102

651-259-3000
1-800-657-3773
www.mnhs.org

Beginning on December 26 and continuing for 6 more days, Kwanzaa is an American holiday season created in 1966 to celebrate African culture through traditional music, stories and the arts. Kwanzaa, a Swahili word, means "first." And so on the first day of the festival, the MHC each year plans an afternoon of family events. These could include storytelling, dance, drumming and always a hands-on African theme children's art activity. One year it was creating a linguist staff from cardboard paper rolls, beads, colored tissues, tapes and trinkets. Fee is $10 for adults, $8 for seniors and $5 for children from 6 to 17. The Minnesota Café located in the MHC serves Kwanzaa theme food, too.

MACY'S CHILDREN'S EVENTS – November & December
700 Nicollet Mall
Minneapolis, 55402

612-375-3018
www.macys.com

SantaLand, in the store's 8th floor auditorium, opens mid-November and continues through December. The 10,000 square-foot area is transformed into a fantasyland of imaginative settings and animated characters with the visitors to it looking and listening as they walk through. Past events have included the staging of Cinderella, Charlie & the Chocolate Factory and A Day in the Life of an Elf.

On certain weekend days during the holiday season, children can have Breakfast with Santa and his Friends. Call for details on dates and breakfast cost or click on Events on the website.

Note: A two-week flower show **www.macys.com/flowershow** held late March and early April co-sponsored with Bachman's is mainly for adults but most children enjoy a short walk-through visit, too. Towers of Flowers was the theme of a previous show. Go during the less crowded evening hours or early in the week.

*NORTHWEST SPORTSHOW – March
Minneapolis Convention Center
1301 S. 2nd Ave.
Minneapolis, 55403

612-335-6000 or 612-335-6025 (infoline)
www.minneapolisconventioncenter.com
www.NorthwestSportshow.com

This show has been an annual event for over 75 years, but in recent years has become a truly family event. Changes have taken place to include entertainment and activities for young visitors. Children can learn more about the outdoors, indoors, as they are encouraged to learn about fishing, hunting safely and bird watching.

Held from Wednesday to Sunday beginning in late March, the show has included a trout pond where a child can fish keeping the catch or returning it to the pond. They can discover the fun of fly fishing by learning to tie a fly and how to fly cast. Admission is $10 for ages 16 and older and free for ages 15 and under with paid adult. Look for discount coupons available at some local stores. Call or visit website for hours.

*THE NUTCRACKER

With many fine Nutcracker ballet productions to choose from presently, a time to attend a performance of this seasonal family treat should be found during even the busiest of December weekends.

The story told begins with a magician bringing toys to children at a Christmas party. Clara receives a nutcracker that later that night comes to life. She then helps him lead the toy soldiers to victory over the invading mice. The nutcracker becomes a prince who then takes Clara to the Kingdom of Sweets for dancing and to be entertained by the Sugar Plum Fairy.

And any one of these productions will provide the same wonderful enchanting entertainment for children of all ages.

*Ballet Minnesota's **The Classic Nutcracker** (651-290-0513) is the traditional version of the ballet with guest dancers from well-known ballet companies. Children's roles are danced by our local Classical Ballet Academy students. Performances are in mid-December at O'Shaughnessy, St. Catherine University, 2004 Randolph Ave., St. Paul, 55105, (651-690-6700). Tickets are $15 to $40. **www.balletminnesota.org**

***Loyce Houlton's Nutcracker Fantasy** has been a favorite for over 50 years. The *New York Times* has called the Minnesota Dance Theatre's (MDT) (612-338-0627) production one of the ten best American Nutcrackers. Performances are held in mid-December at the Historic State Theatre, 805 Hennepin Ave., Minneapolis, 55402. Tickets are $40 to $60. **www.mndance.org/site**

***Stillwater Nutcracker** is also a traditional performance. However, it has narration that makes it more understandable and enjoyable for younger children. Professional dancers perform with hundreds of St. Croix Ballet students some as young as five. Performances are on the weekend following Thanksgiving at the Stillwater Area High School Auditorium, 5701 Stillwater Blvd. N., Oak Park Heights, 55082, (651-439-2820). Tickets are $15. **www.stcroixballet.com**

PHILIPPINE DAY – March
Rice Park
Landmark Center
75 W. 5th St.
St. Paul, 55102

651-292-3225 (infoline)
www.csfamn.org

On a Sunday afternoon in late March, Philippine food, folk music and dance can be enjoyed at the Landmark Center. The festival is sponsored by the Cultural Society of Filipino Americans in the Twin Cities. Arts and crafts are for sale and there are interesting exhibits, too.

ST. PATRICK'S DAY PARADE & CELEBRATION – March
St. Patrick's Day Association
PO Box 2303
St. Paul, 55102

651-256-2155 (infoline)
www.stpatsassoc.org

St. Patrick's Day is March 17th and is celebrated in St. Paul with a Walking Parade beginning at noon. Check out the parade map and route on the website.

The St. Paul organizers think only New York City and Boston have larger parades than ours. However, they fondly think of ours as the largest Baby Buggy parade. This is a family event with children riding in decorated wagons and baby strollers. In fact, anyone can march in the parade as long as he or she is wearing something green.

However, advance registration is required by the association to participate in the parade. The registration form is available on their website.

In one of the many parades we have attended, the O'Any Bodies family marched. And a grade school kazoo band could be heard playing When Irish Eyes Are Smiling.

In St. Paul, the parade starts about noon and winds through the downtown area. Consult their website or the St. Paul newspaper for the parade route and starting time.

*SCOTTISH RAMBLE – February
Rice Park
Landmark Center
75 W. 5th St.
St. Paul, 55102

651-292-3225 (infoline)
www.scottishramble.org

On a weekend in February, our local Scottish heritage is promoted with pipe bands, Celtic music and highland dances. Children are encouraged to sit near the performance stage and have been known to enjoy the music so much they stand up and start dancing, too. And this is fine with the performers.

There are displays of bagpipes, Scottish customs and clan information. Scottish food and crafts are sold. Admission is $5 for adults and $3 for seniors and children.

*SHAKESPEARE CLASSIC – January or March or April
Guthrie Theater
818 2nd St. S.
Minneapolis, 55415

612-377-2224
www.guthrietheater.org/shakespeare

During a Guthrie production of a Shakespeare play, young people ages 10 to 17 can attend a one-time, annual special matinee performance. In the past, the performance has been on a Sunday in January or March or April. The event month is dependent upon when the Guthrie schedules their Shakespeare play performances. Tickets are available well in advance of the Classic performance, are very reasonably priced at $10 and go quickly. This is a way to introduce families to the wonderful world of live theater at our Guthrie. To learn more about the current year Classic and determine whether the play is age-appropriate, refer to the Play Guide on the website.

In the lobby upon arrival an excellent program with notes about the costumes, set design, lights and music as well as facts about William Shakespeare and especially written for young people is received. Following the play, attendees are invited to meet members of the cast. Refreshments are served, too. Visit the Guthrie website for an announcement of when the Shakespeare Classic program is to be held each year.

URBAN EXPEDITIONS – January - April
Rice Park
Landmark Center
75 W. 5th St.
St. Paul, 55102

651-292-3276
www.landmarkcenter.org

Children experience the cultures of countries outside the United States without leaving St. Paul at Urban Expeditions events. Each child is given a passport at his or hers first visit. It can then be used for "entrance" to future visits. On select Sundays at 1 PM January through April, the music and dance and an art activity of the featured country is explored. Past country visits have included Nepal, Chile and Ghana. Call or check website for specific future dates and countries scheduled for travel.

WINTER CARNIVAL – January
St. Paul Festival & Heritage Foundation
429 Landmark Center
75 W. 5th St.
St. Paul, 55102

651-223-4700 (infoline)
www.winter-carnival.com

The first Winter Carnival was held in 1886 as a celebration of the end of winter and the beginning of spring. Each year since, Vulcan on the last day of the carnival tries to dethrone King Boreas to bring about spring-like weather. The fiery Vulcan always wins but warm weather never arrives as predicted by his victory. Another tradition at each year's carnival is the spectacular ice carving competition now held in Rice Park.

Events children might like to participate in include the medallion treasure hunt, snow maze and sledding hill.

Winter Carnival activities begin the last Friday in January and continue through the following week ending on Saturday. The King Boreas Grande Day parade is at 2:30 PM on the first Saturday of the celebration. In this parade, the popular Hi-lex bleach gnomes marching unit, fondly know as the drips of bleach, receive lots of cheers. The Torchlight Parade is at 5:30 PM on the last Saturday.

This is the oldest winter celebration in North America and we really enjoy it! Check local newspapers or visit their website for all the many scheduled official events and their current locations.

NOTES

CATEGORIES INDEX

Animals

Art Activities & Centers

Birthday Parties

Camps & Classes

Fairs & Festivals

Film Programs

Gardens & Flower Shows

Heritage & Nationality Culture

Historical Sites & Societies

Libraries

.

Museums

Music

Nature Centers & Programs

Observation Decks & Platforms

Parades

Parks & Recreational Centers

Playgrounds

Puppet Shows & Storytime Programs

Sports

Theaters & Shows

Tours

Transportation & Rides